KARIN HOCHSTATTER

gegengerade

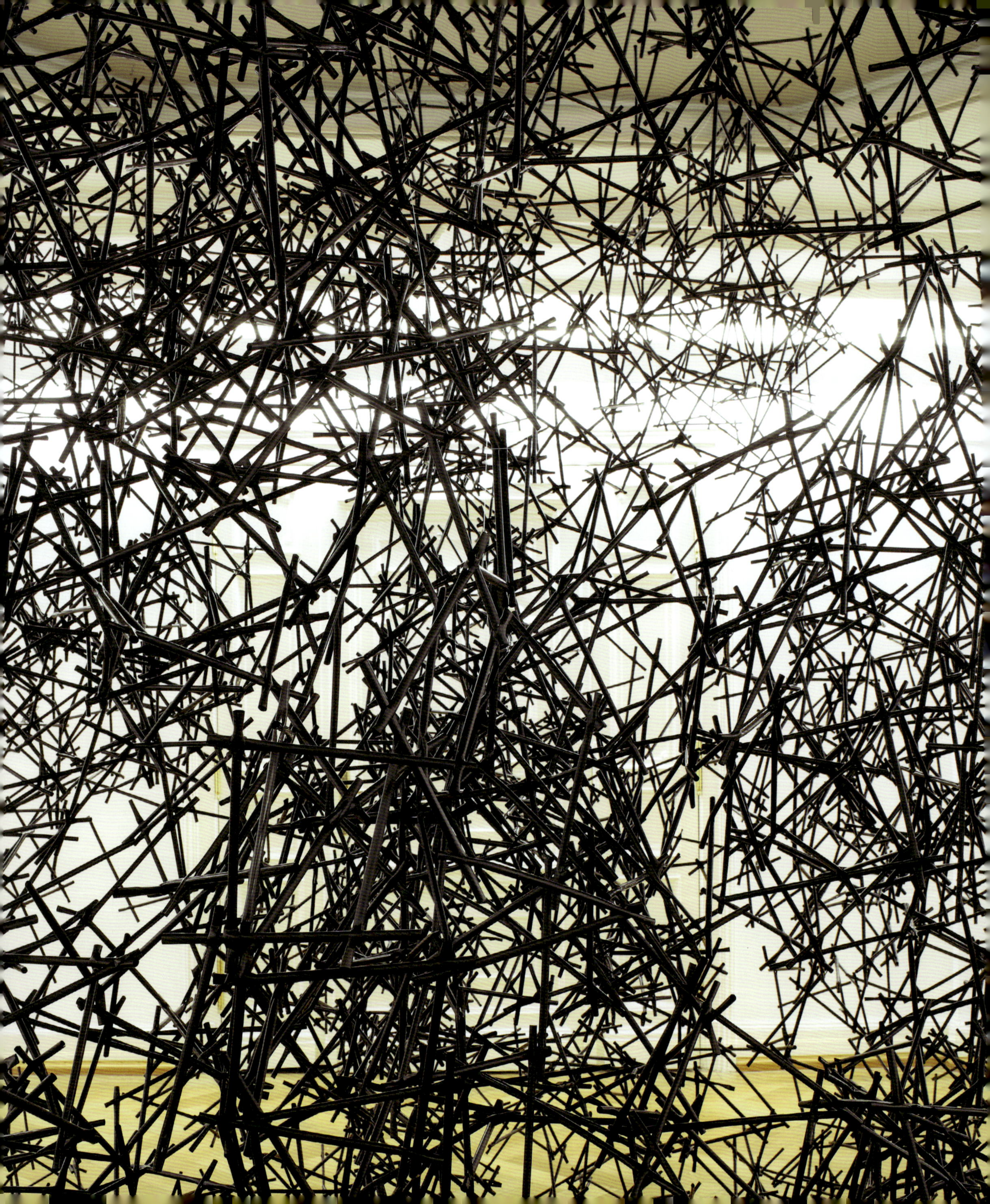

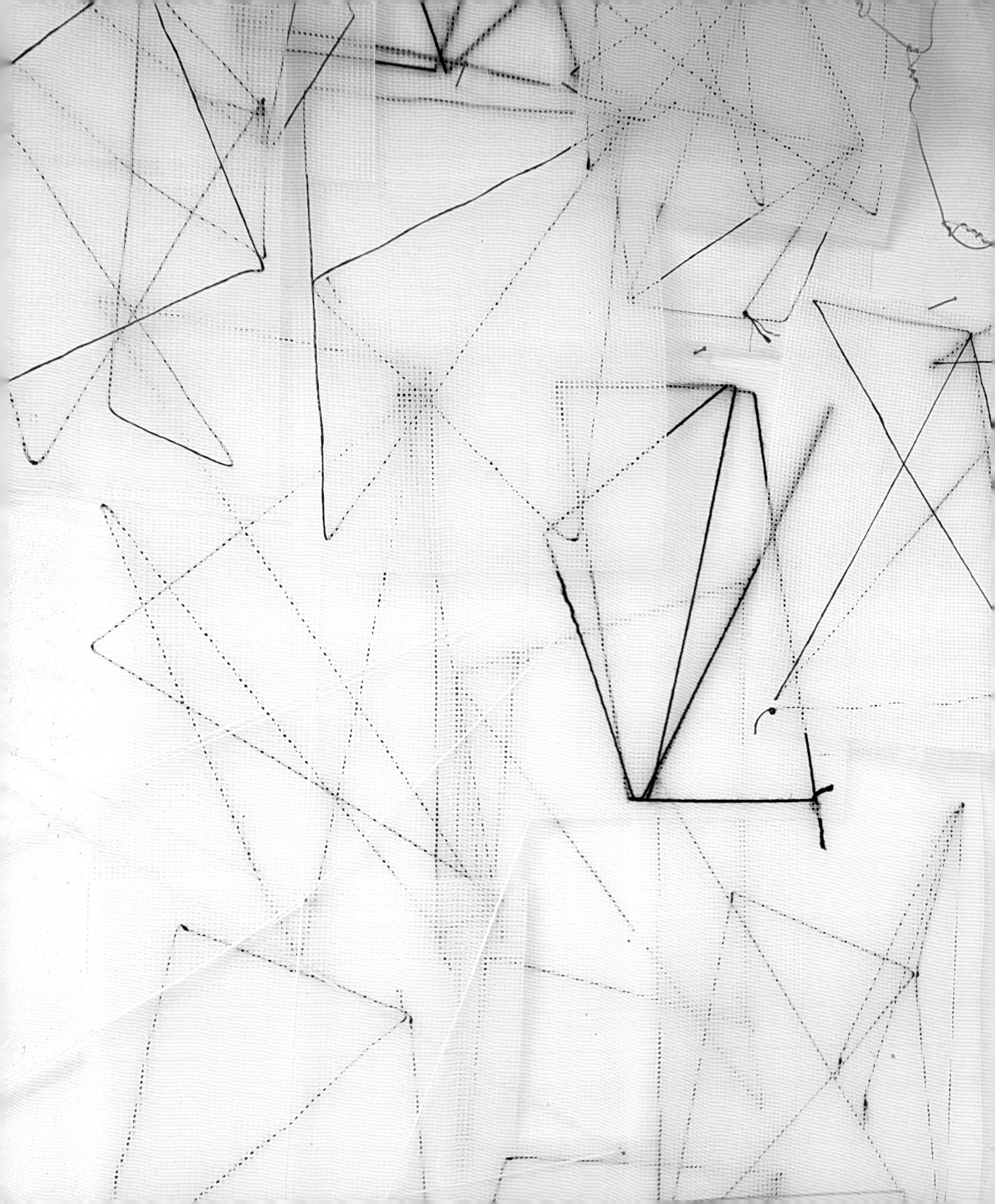

KARIN HOCHSTATTER

gegengerade

edition cantz

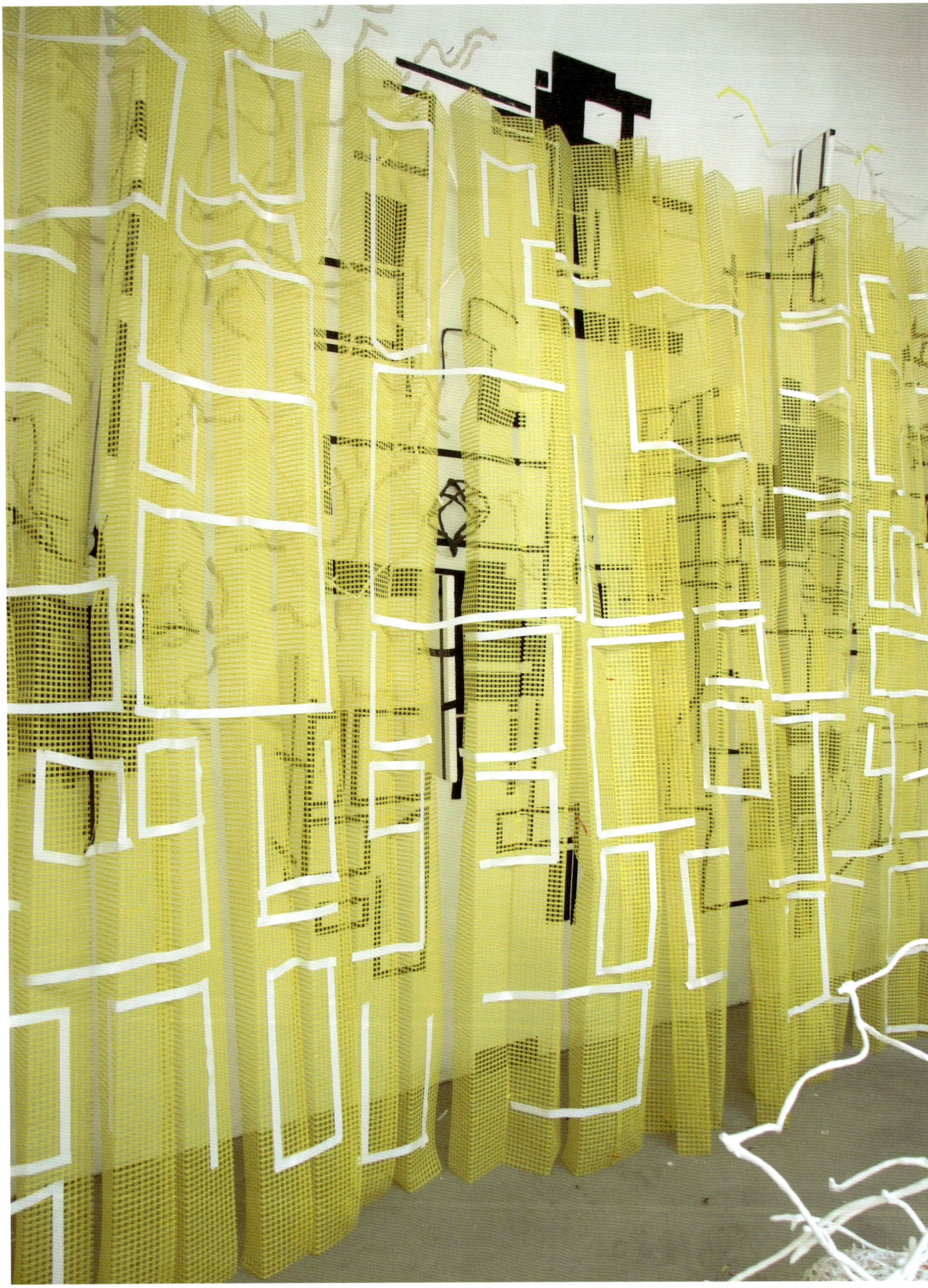

Inhalt | Contents

Right: *DS,* 2012, (detail), installation, drinking straws, dimension variable

Following page: *CC3*, 2015, wall installation, paper, cord, spray paint, metal edges, 300 x 1000 x 100 cm

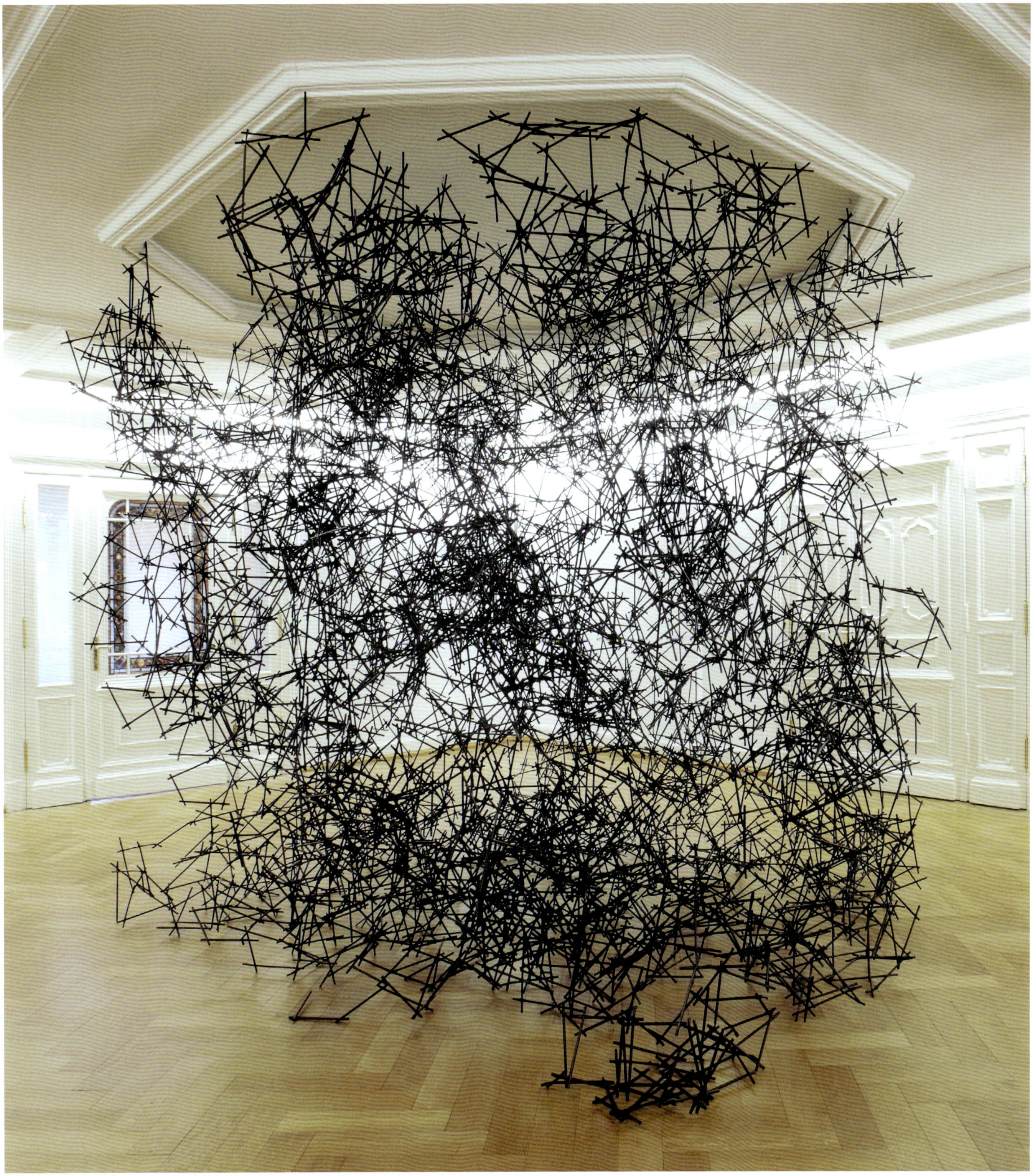

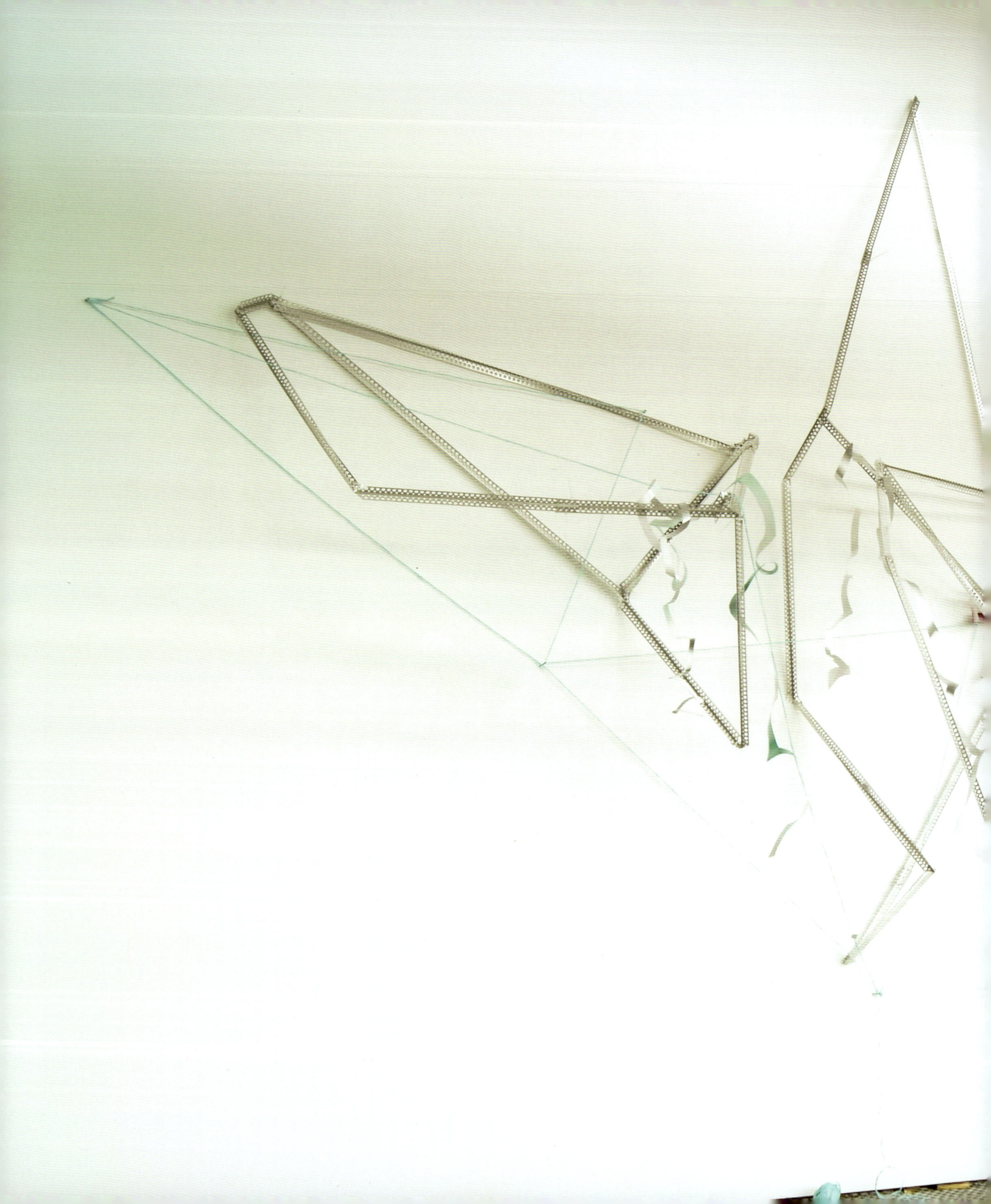

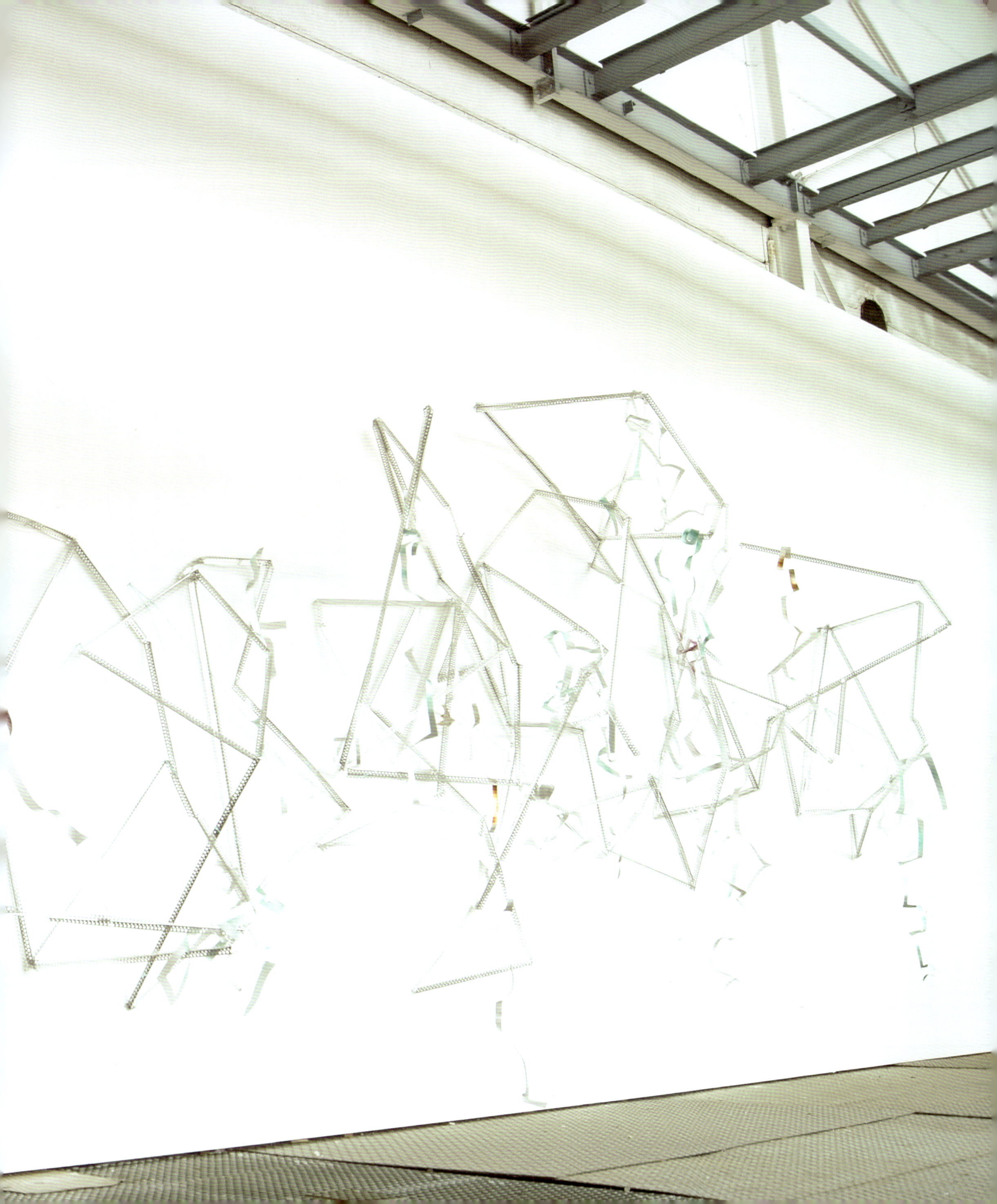

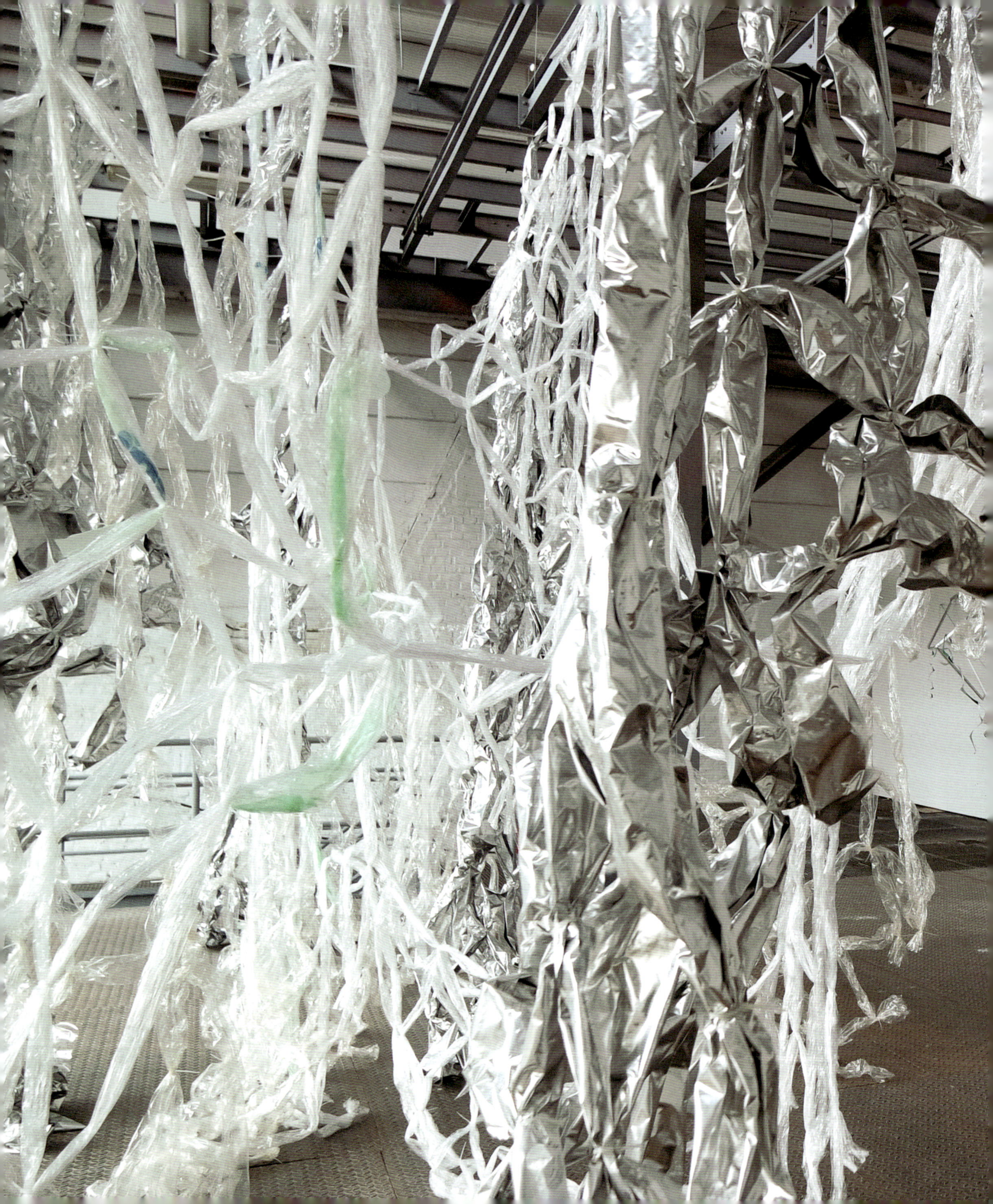

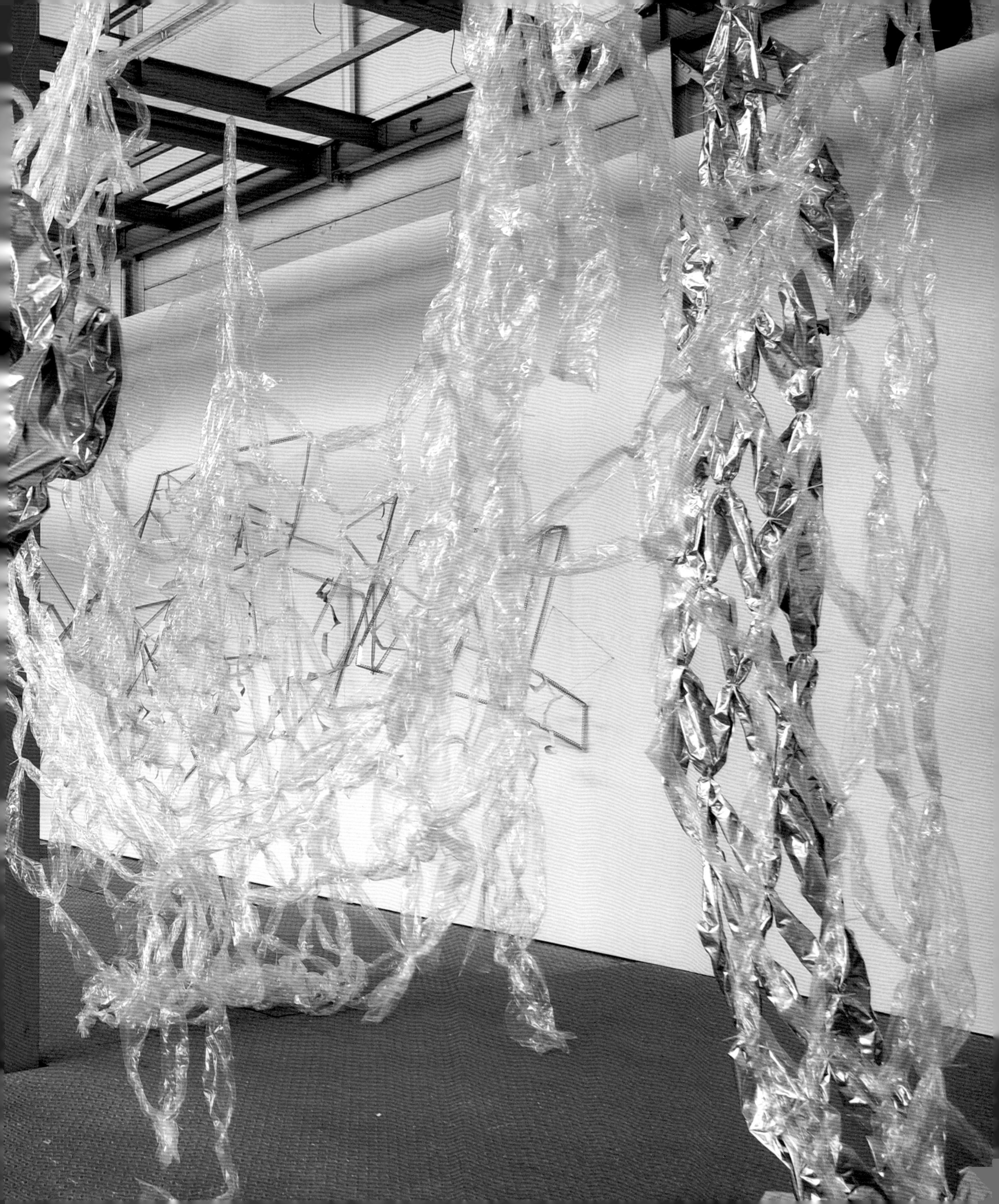

Previous page: *CC2*, 2015, various foils and packaging materials, dimension variable

Right: *CC1*, 2015, wire, photocopies, paper, 350 x 170 x 45 cm

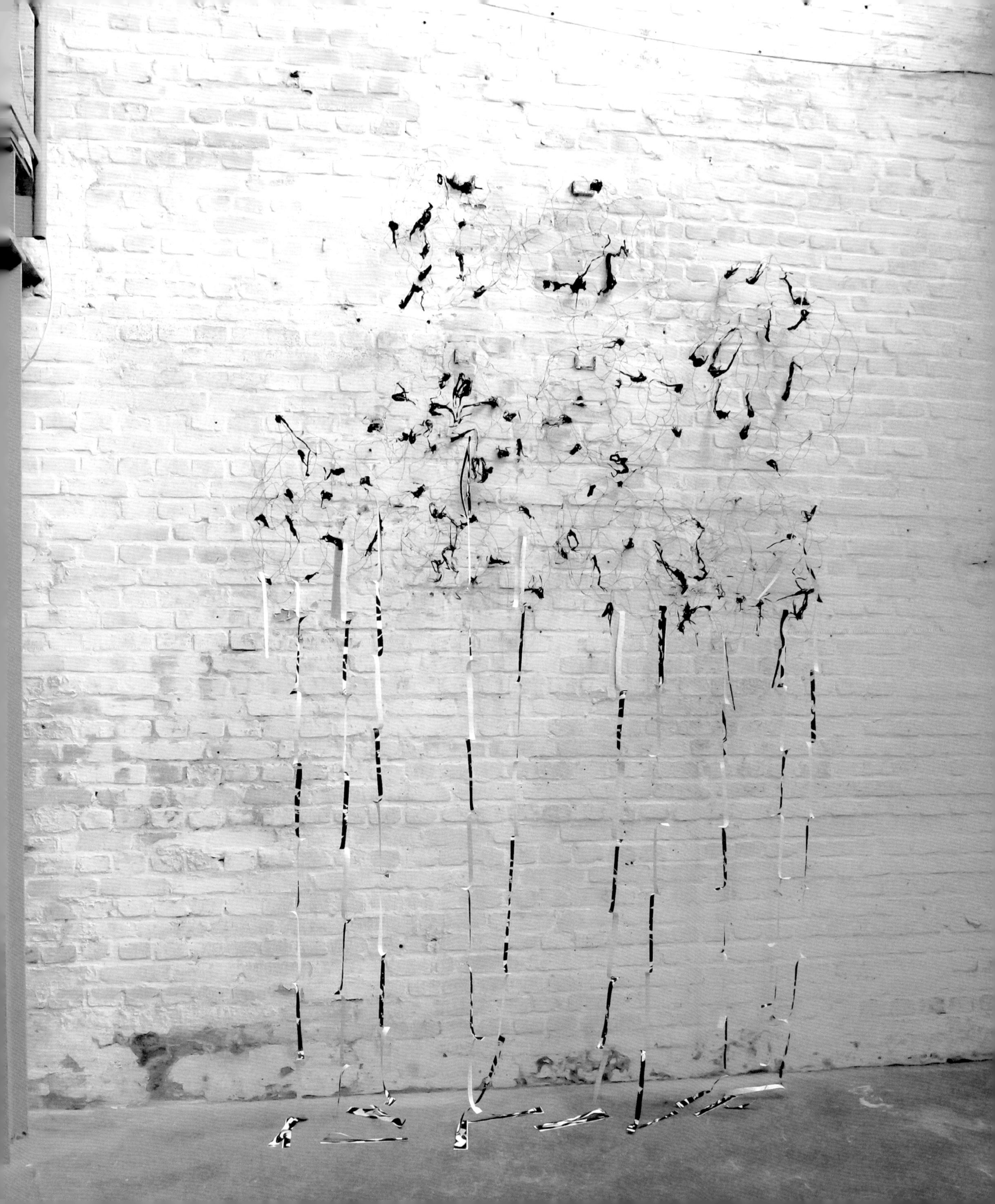

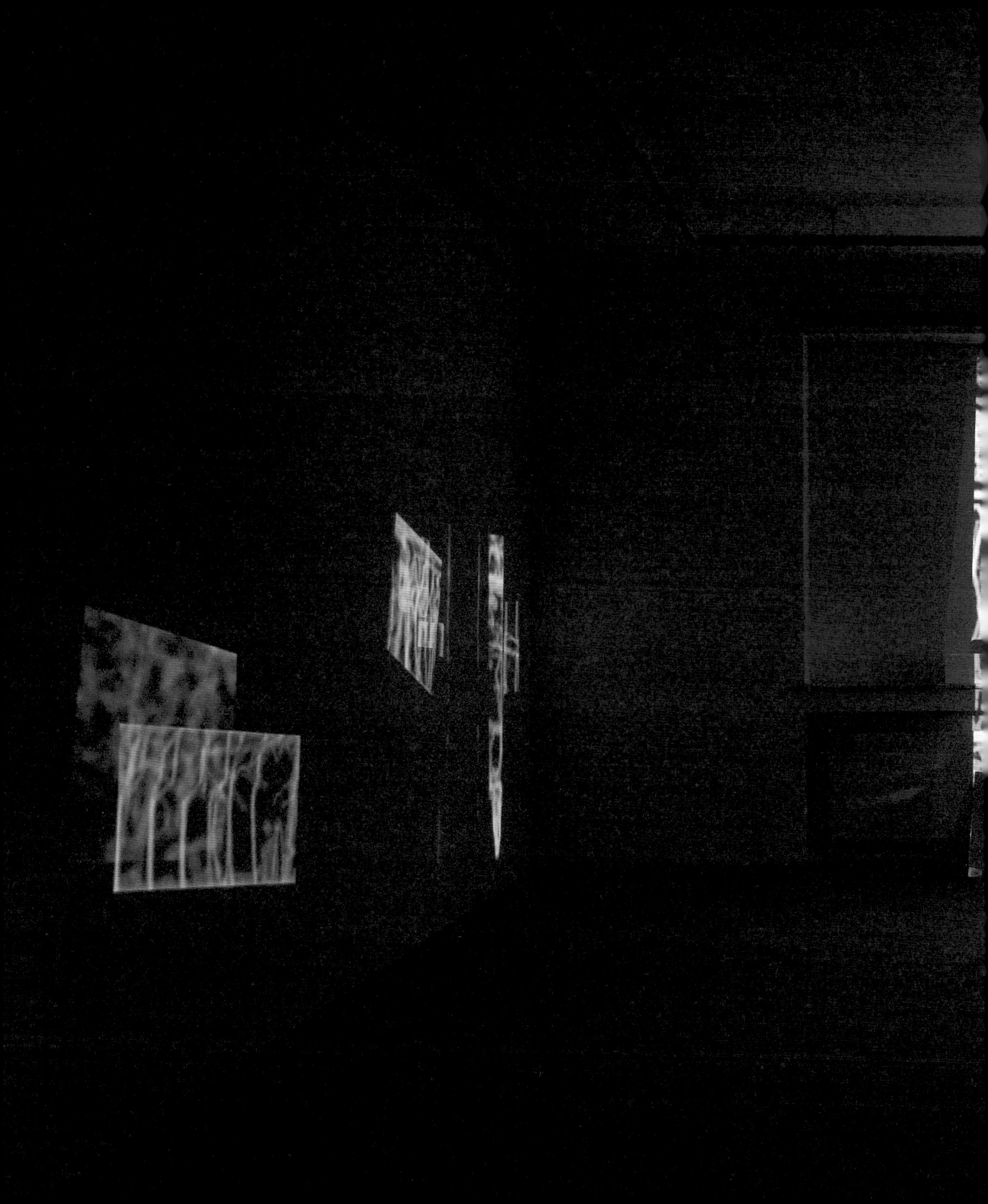

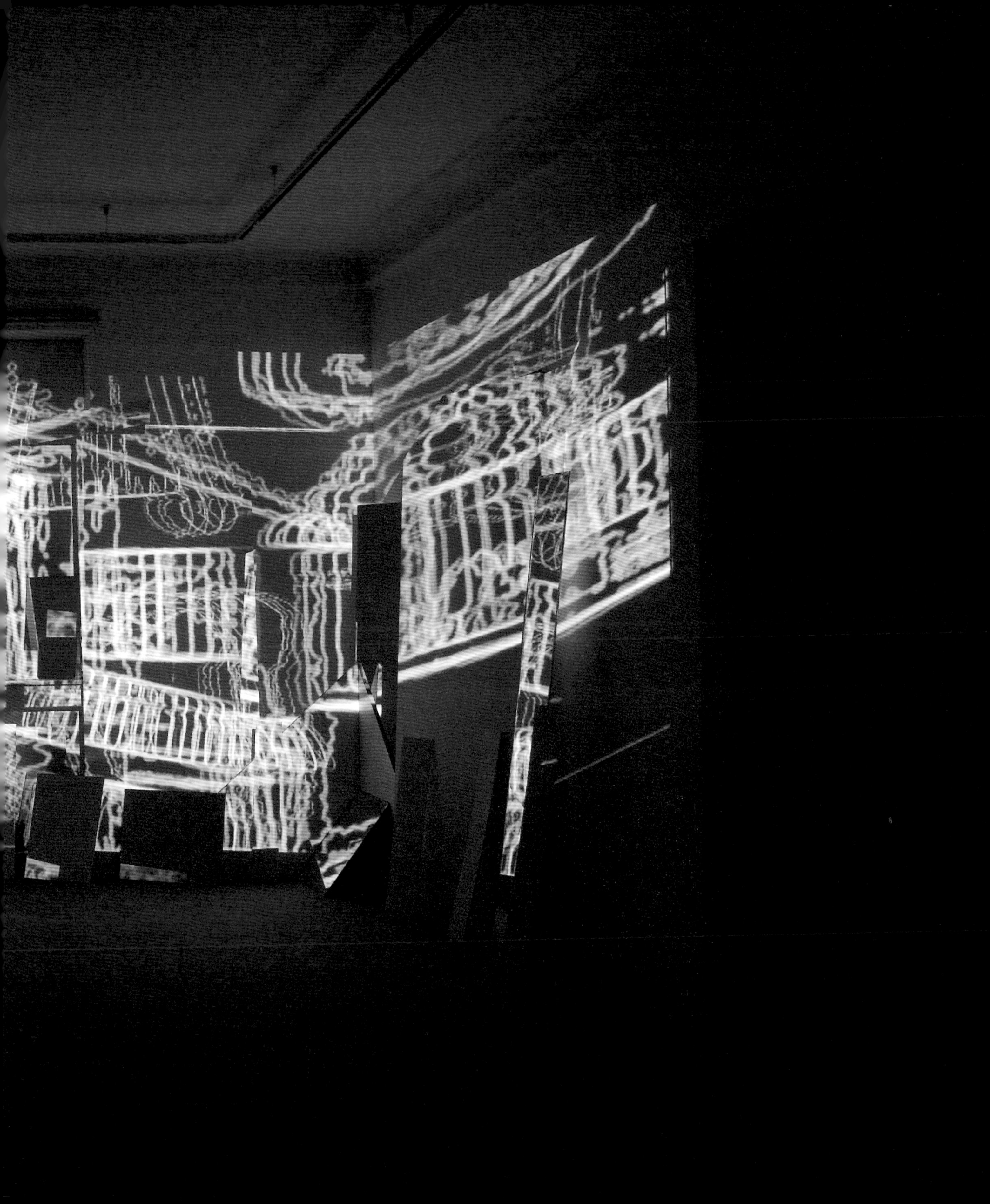

Previous page: *Zanfour,* 2012, video loop 4:25 min, colour, sound, 4:3, mirrors, wooden panels

Right: *Phi*, 2016, video projection, 2 min loop, sound, colour, HD 16:9, various foils, nets, curtains

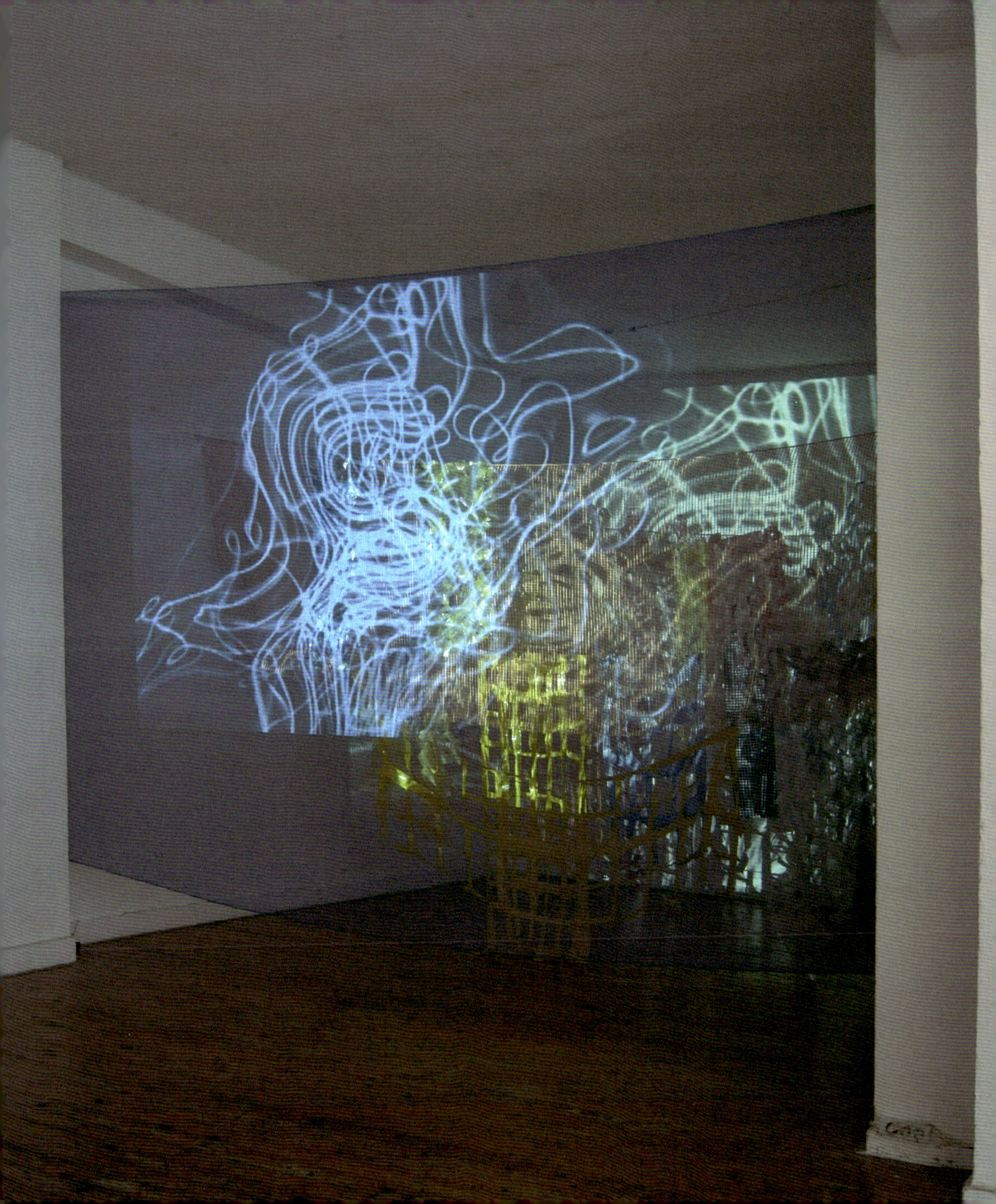

Thomas Wallraff

Per se – Gegengerade

„Man ist um den Preis Künstler, dass man das, was alle Nicht-Künstler ‚Form' nennen, als Inhalt, als ‚die Sache selbst' empfindet."[1] Dieses Notat Friedrich Nietzsches aus der Spätphase seines Werks trifft die künstlerische Haltung Karin Hochstatters in ihrem Kern. Es geht ihr um die Sache selbst: Kunst. Kunst, die per se, also „durch sich", „von selbst", ihre Wirkungen entfaltet. Kunst, in der es keine Trennung zwischen formalen Qualitäten und vermeintlich davon zu unterscheidenden Inhalten gibt. Diese Haltung ist alles andere als eine Selbstverständlichkeit. Zumal derzeit Arbeiten der zeitgenössischen Kunst, sei es durch die Produzenten selbst, sei es durch sie umgebende Kommentatoren, fortwährend mit Bezügen, Bedeutungen, Inhalten versehen werden. Das Problem hierbei: Diese Inhalte werden von außen in die Kunst injiziert, in den Arbeiten finden sie oft keine hinreichende formale Entsprechung und noch seltener erschließen sie sich per se (von selbst), also allein durch aufmerksame Wahrnehmung des Werks an sich. Das führt gerade bei im Vorfeld umfassend informierten, aber gleichwohl kritischen Betrachtern oftmals zu Enttäuschungen. Die eigentlichen Arbeiten erscheinen im Vergleich mit den ihnen zugesprochenen Inhalten, den ihnen zur Seite gestellten theoretischen Konstrukten in vielen Fällen eher matt. Bertolt Brecht benannte dieses Phänomen als „Inhaltismus"[2] und entgegnete so dem Vorwurf des „Formalismus", der den Künsten in ästhetisch-politischen Debatten von rechts wie links bereits seit den 1950er-Jahren gemacht wird. Natürlich gilt nach wie vor das Diktum Goethes: „Man sieht nur, was man weiß."[3] Aber durch ihre Arbeit erwidert Karin Hochstatter implizit: „Was nützt alles Vorwissen, wenn man letztendlich nichts zu sehen bekommt?" Mit L'art pour l'art hat das rein gar nichts zu tun. Eher schon mit L'art pour les voyants – einer Kunst für Sehende, einer Kunst, die auf das Sehen vertraut und es herausfordert. Das Sehen aber ist das Kernstück der bildenden Kunst, wie ihrer Rezeption. Wer dem zustimmen kann, bereit ist, sich hoher visueller Komplexität zu stellen und der Auffassung ist, dass ein Kunstwerk etwas Neues, Eigenes, so noch nie Gesehenes verkörpert, jenseits von externen Inhalten, die sich per se gar nicht repräsentieren lassen: Der wird in den Arbeiten der Künstlerin Karin Hochstatter potenziell infinite Seherfahrungen machen können.

Dabei hat man den besten Blick auf ihr Schaffen von der Gegengerade. Während auf der Haupttribüne – dort wo das etablierte Publikum und die medialen Multiplikatoren Platz nehmen – das Geschehen vornehmlich analytisch betrachtet wird, nach dem Sinn des Ganzen oder doch wenigstens nach Spielsystem und -philosophie gefragt wird, sieht man von der Gegengerade alles genau andersherum. Hier steht die Begeisterung für die Form und Schönheit des Spiels (der Kunst) im Vordergrund. Drüben wird kritisiert, auf der Gegengerade lässt man sich mitreißen.

Letztlich deutet auch eine Analyse des Wortes und Titels „Gegengerade" auf eine gewisse Gegenposition hin, gibt aber vor allem einen Einblick in das künstlerische Tun von Karin Hochstatter. Das Wort ist gebildet aus dem Präfix „gegen" und dem Substantiv „Gerade". Laut dem zehnbändigen *Duden. Das große Wörterbuch der deutschen Sprache*[4] bedeutet das Affix „gegen" in Verbindung mit einem Substantiv: „[...] dass etwas in Opposition zum Üblichen, Etablierten steht [...] drückt [...] die Erwiderung von etwas aus [...] kennzeichnet [...] etwas als gegenüberliegend, in entgegengesetzter Richtung verlaufend [...] drückt [...] aus, dass etwas (zur Entkräftung, Bekämpfung) entgegengestellt, entgegengesetzt wird [... und] drückt [...] die Kontrolle von etwas aus". Das Substantiv „Gerade" als Letztglied der Wortbildung „Gegengerade" hat im Deutschen drei Bedeutungen: 1. eine keine Krümmung aufweisende, prinzipiell unendliche Linie, 2. der ohne Biegung verlaufende Teil einer Rennstrecke oder Laufbahn, 3. ein ohne Auf-, Ab-, oder seitlichen Schwung direkt ins Ziel geführter Faustschlag. Wortgeschichtlich ist die „Gerade" übrigens eine Substantivierung des Adjektivs und Adverbs „gerade", welches im Mittelhochdeutschen (dem Deutsch des Hochmittelalters, etwa zwischen 1050 und 1350) die Bedeutungen „schnell bei der Hand", „rasch", „gewandt" besaß.[5] Wer einmal die Gelegenheit hatte, Karin Hochstatter gerade beim Aufbau von raumbezogenen, installativen Arbeiten zu beobachten, dem werden wahrscheinlich ganz ähnliche Attribute einfallen. Mit schneller, sicherer Hand errichtet sie ihre lichten Gebilde. Alles erscheint rasch, wie eine Skizze, hingeworfen – fragil, expansiv. Und doch ist es zugleich von überraschender Standhaftigkeit, Haltung, ruhend in sich. Mit geringem Materialaufwand (in Hinsicht auf Schwere, Menge und Wertigkeit) werden selbst ausladende Räume verändert, neu apostrophiert, mitunter auch beherrscht, falls dies notwendig ist. Mit feinen Fäden wird sogar Riesenhaftes gebunden oder in der Schwebe gehalten, wollene Schnüre weisen nicht den Weg heraus, sondern ziehen hinein in Labyrinthe des Sehens. All das ohne rhetorische Abschweifungen oder Schwünge; direkte, trockene, technisch saubere Schläge – immer auf die Augen zielend.

[1] Friedrich Nietzsche, *Der Wille zur Macht II* (Kap. IV, Nr. 818), Leipzig 1922.

[2] Siehe auch Martin Hatzius, „Unten links" in: *neues deutschland*, Ausgabe vom 22.8.2013, S. 1.

[3] Goethe in einem Brief an Friedrich von Müller vom 24.4.1819. Zit. nach Johann Wolfgang von Goethe, *Gedenkausgabe der Werke. Briefe und Gespräche*, 24 Bde., Zürich, Stuttgart 1948ff., Bd. 13, S. 142.

[4] *Duden. Das große Wörterbuch der deutschen Sprache*, 10 Bde., Mannheim, Leipzig, Wien, Zürich 1999.

[5] Siehe auch Wolfgang Pfeifer (Hrsg.), *Etymologisches Wörterbuch des Deutschen*, 2 Bde., Berlin [2]1993.

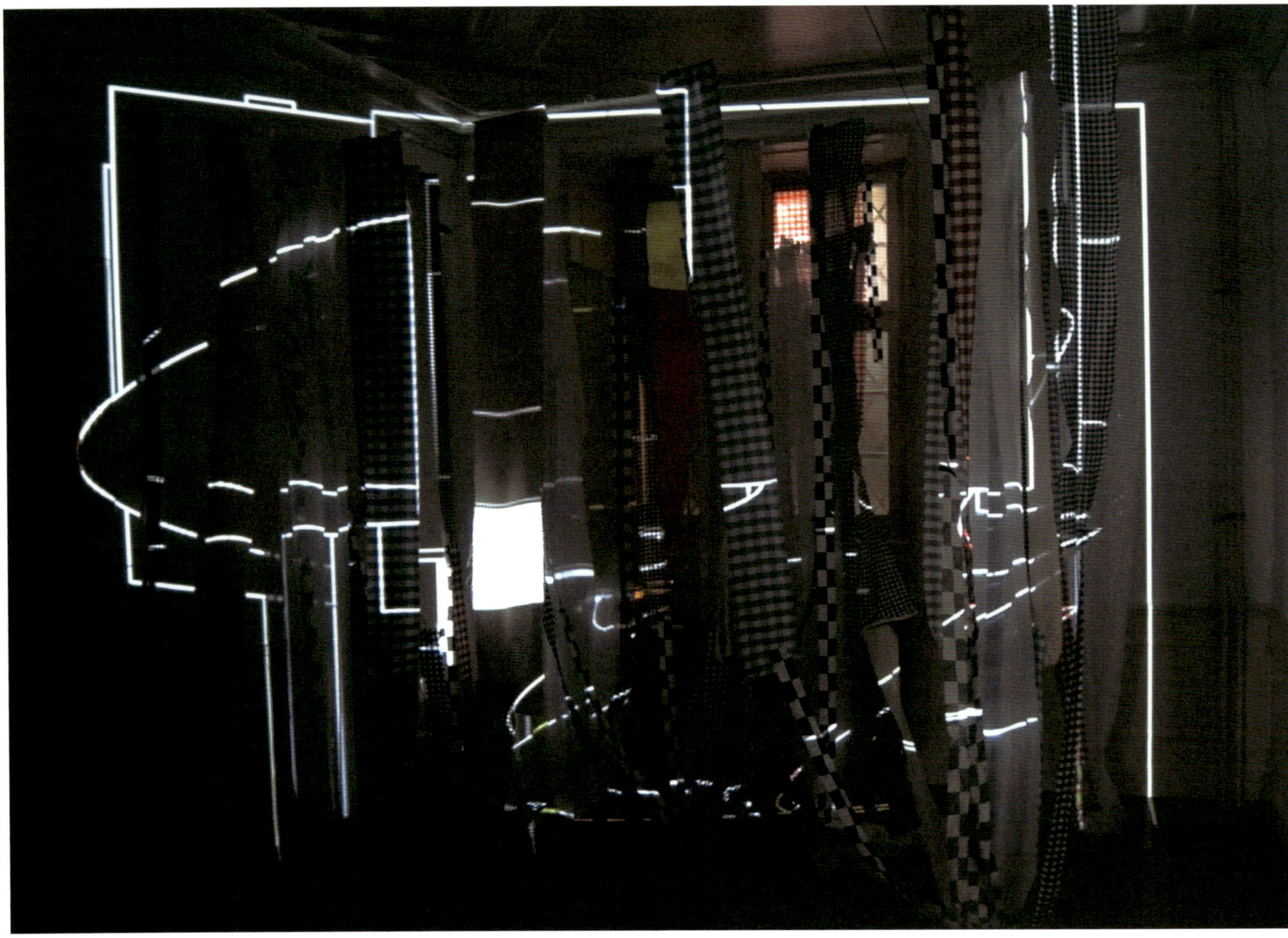

Ringsum, 2016, video loop 2:20 min, colour, without sound, 4:3, checked fabrics, curtains

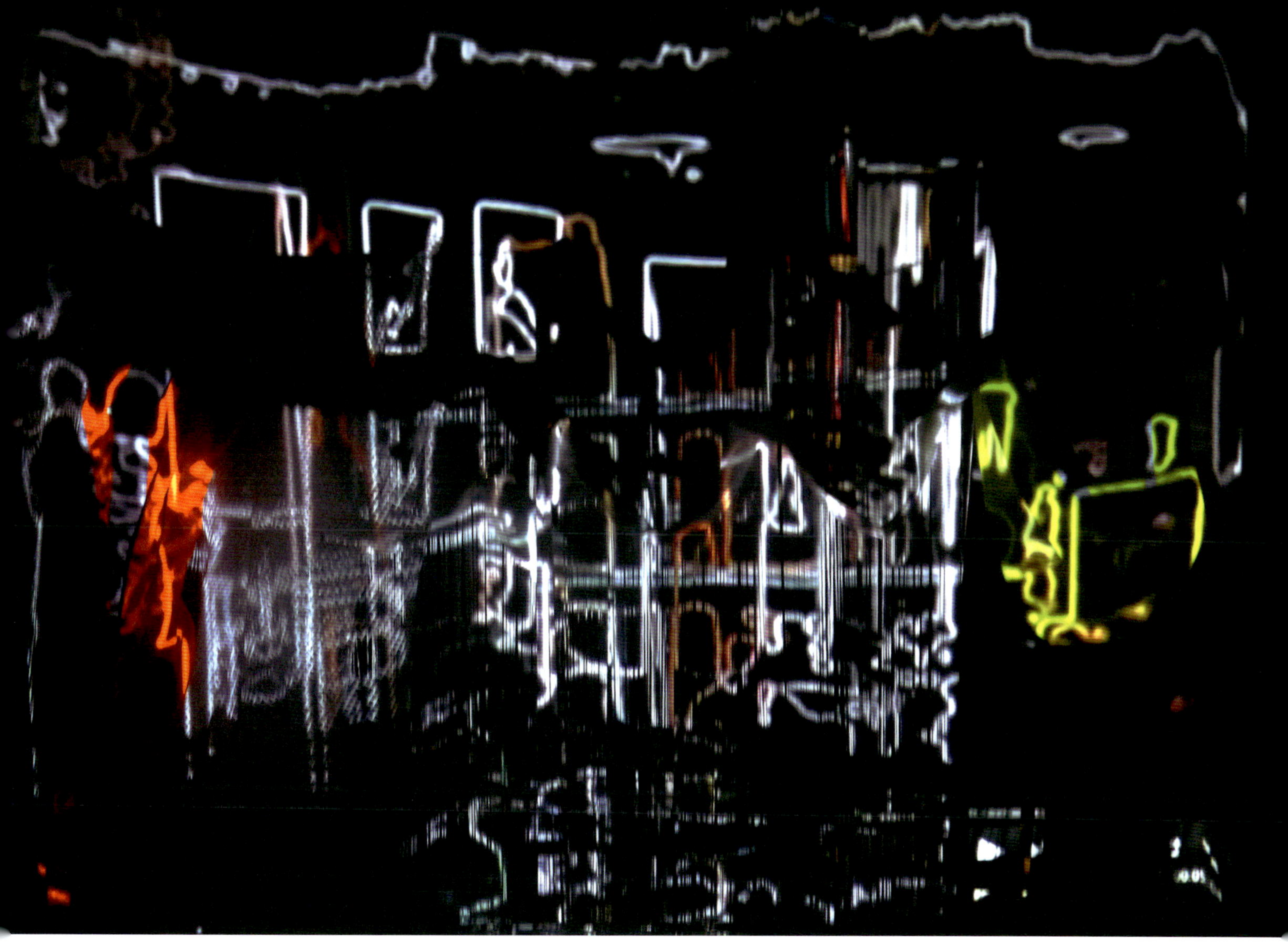

Skop, 2013, installation in a construction wagon, video loop 8:21 min, sound, colour, 4:3, high visibility vests, thread curtains, fluorescent materials

Thomas Wallraff

Per Se – Back Straight

"One is an artist at the price of perceiving what all non-artists call 'form' as content, as 'the thing itself'."[1] This annotation by Friedrich Nietzsche from the late phase of his oeuvre reflects the artistic attitude of Karin Hochstatter at its core. She is concerned with the cause itself: art. Art that unfolds its impacts per se, that is, "by itself", "spontaneously". Art in which there is no separation between formal qualities and supposedly distinguishable contents. This attitude is anything but a matter of course. Especially since nowadays, works of contemporary art are constantly being provided with references, meanings and contents, whether by the producers themselves or by the commentators surrounding them. The problem here is that these contents are injected into the art from the outside, they often find no sufficient formal correspondence in the works, and even more rarely are they revealed per se (spontaneously), i.e., solely through attentive perception of the work itself. This often leads to disappointment, especially among viewers who are comprehensively informed but at the same time critical. In many cases, the actual works appear rather dull in view of the contents assigned to them, the theoretical constructs flanking them. Bertolt Brecht called this phenomenon "contentism"[2] and thus countered the accusation of "formalism", which has been made of the arts in aesthetic-political debates from both the right and left since the 1950s. Of course, Goethe's dictum still applies: "You only see what you know."[3] But through her work, Karin Hochstatter implicitly replies: "What good is all prior knowledge if you do not get to see anything in the end?" This has nothing to do with l'art pour l'art. It has more to do with l'art pour les voyants – an art for the sighted, an art that trusts in seeing and challenges it. Indeed, seeing is the core of visual art, and lies at the heart of its reception. Those who can agree with this, who are willing to face high visual complexity and are of the opinion that a work of art embodies something new, something personal, something never seen before, beyond external contents that per se cannot be represented at all – those people will be able to make potentially infinite visual experiences in the works of the artist Karin Hochstatter.

The best view of her work is gleaned from the back straight. While on the main grandstand – where the established audience and the media multipliers take their seats – the events are primarily viewed analytically, questions are asked about the meaning of the whole or at least about the underlying system and philosophy of play, one sees everything the other way round from the back straight. Here, the focus is on enthusiasm for the form and beauty of the play (of the art). Over there, criticism reigns, while on the back straight people get carried away.

Finally, an analysis of the German word and title for back straight, "Gegengerade", also points to a certain counter position, but above all it gives an insight into the artistic activity of Karin Hochstatter. The word is formed with the prefix "gegen" ("against"/"back") and the noun "Gerade" ("straight"/"straight line"). According to the ten-volume *Duden. Das große Wörterbuch der deutschen Sprache*[4] (the German language dictionary), in connection with a noun the affix "gegen" means "[...] that something stands in opposition to the usual, established [...] expresses [...] the reply of something [...] marks [...] something as opposite, running in opposite direction [...] expresses [...] that something (for debilitation, combat) is set against, is opposed [... and] expresses [...] the control of something". The noun "Gerade" as the last element of the compound noun "Gegengerade" has three meanings in German: first, a basically infinite line with no curvature; second, the part of a race track that runs without curvature; third, a punch that hits the target directly without any up, down or lateral swing. In terms of etymology, by the way, "Gerade" is a substantiation of the adjective and adverb "gerade", which in Middle High German (the German of the High Middle Ages, between c. 1050 and 1350) could mean "quick off the mark", "rapid" and "versatile".[5] Anyone who has ever had the opportunity to observe Karin Hochstatter in the construction of space-related, installative works will probably come up with very similar attributes. Facile, with a sure hand, she builds her light structures. Everything appears quickly, like a sketch, thrown down – fragile, expansive. And yet, at the same time it is of surprising constancy, posture, resting in itself. With little material expenditure (in terms of weight, quantity and value), even expansive spaces are changed, re-apostrophized and sometimes controlled, if necessary. Even seemingly gigantic objects are bound with fine threads or held in suspension; woollen cords do not point the way out, but draw into labyrinths of seeing. All this unfolds without rhetorical digressions or swings: direct, dry, technically clean blows – always aiming straight at the eyes.

[1] Nietzsche, Friedrich, *Der Wille zur Macht II* (chap. IV, no. 818), (Leipzig, 1922).
[2] See also Hatzius, Martin, *"Unten links"* in *neues deutschland*, issue from 22.8.2013, p. 1.
[3] Goethe in a letter to Friedrich von Müller, dated 24.4.1819. Quoted after Goethe, Johann Wolfgang von, *Gedenkausgabe der Werke, Briefe und Gespräche*, 24 vols. (Zurich, Stuttgart, 1948 et seq.), vol. 13, p. 142.
[4] *Duden. Das große Wörterbuch der deutschen Sprache*, 10 vols. (Mannheim, Leipzig, Vienna, Zurich, 1999).
[5] See also Pfeifer, Wolfgang (ed.), *Etymologisches Wörterbuch des Deutschen*, 2 vols. (Berlin, 1993[2]).

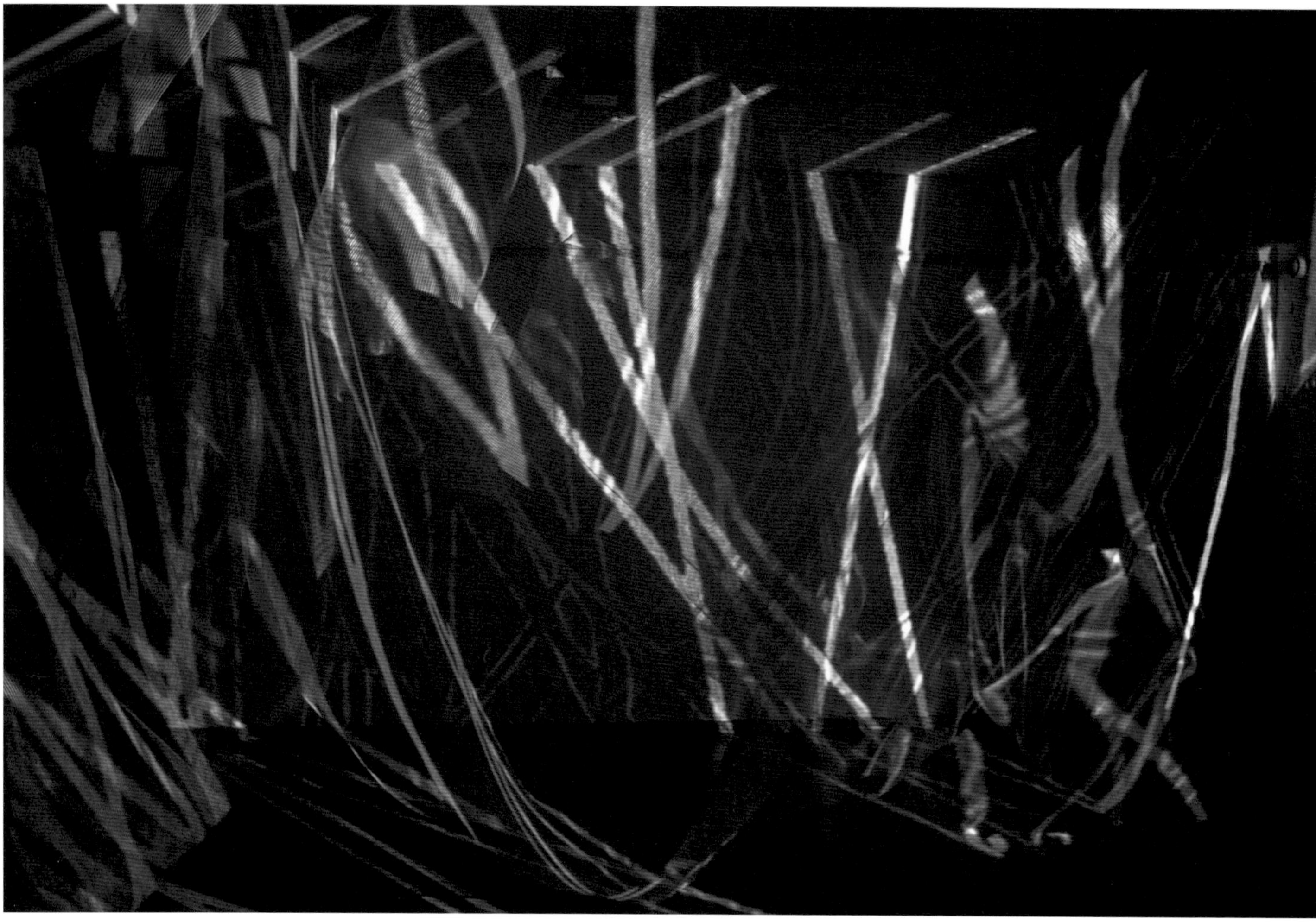

"Je prends aux serieux les phantômes", 2016, video loop 4 min, colour, sound, HD 16:9, construction nets

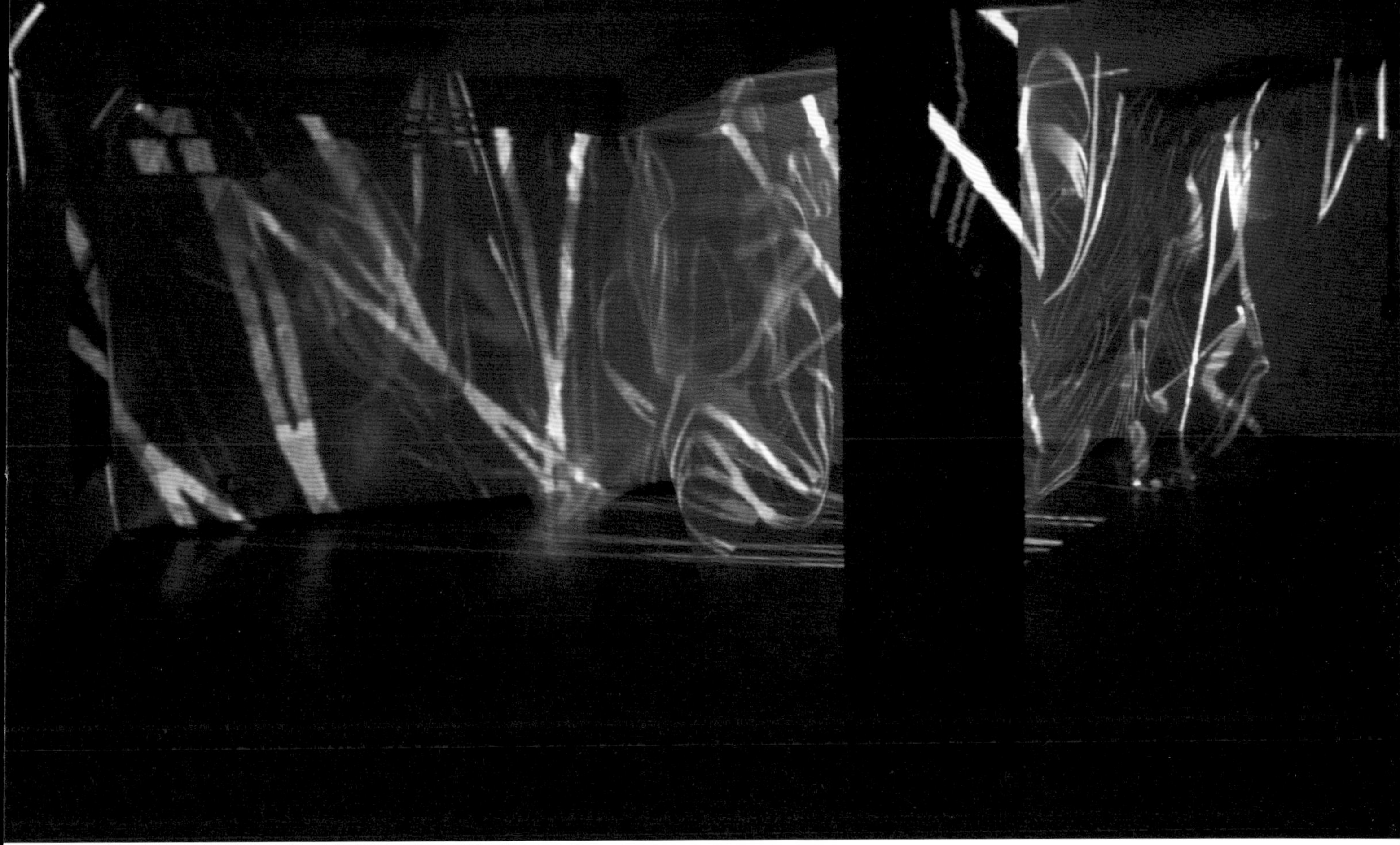

BIAB, 2012, video loop 7 min, colour, without sound, 4:3, thread curtain

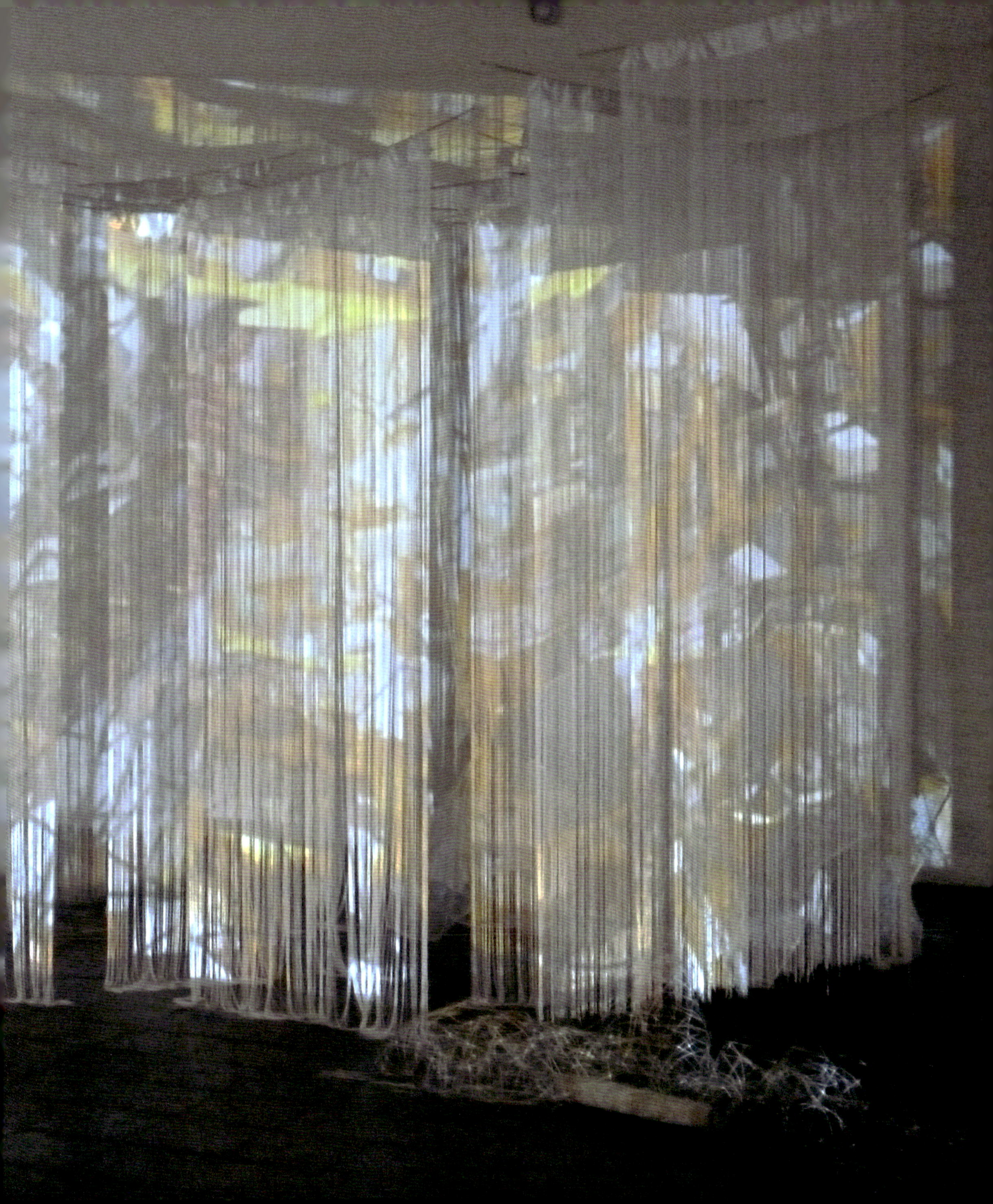

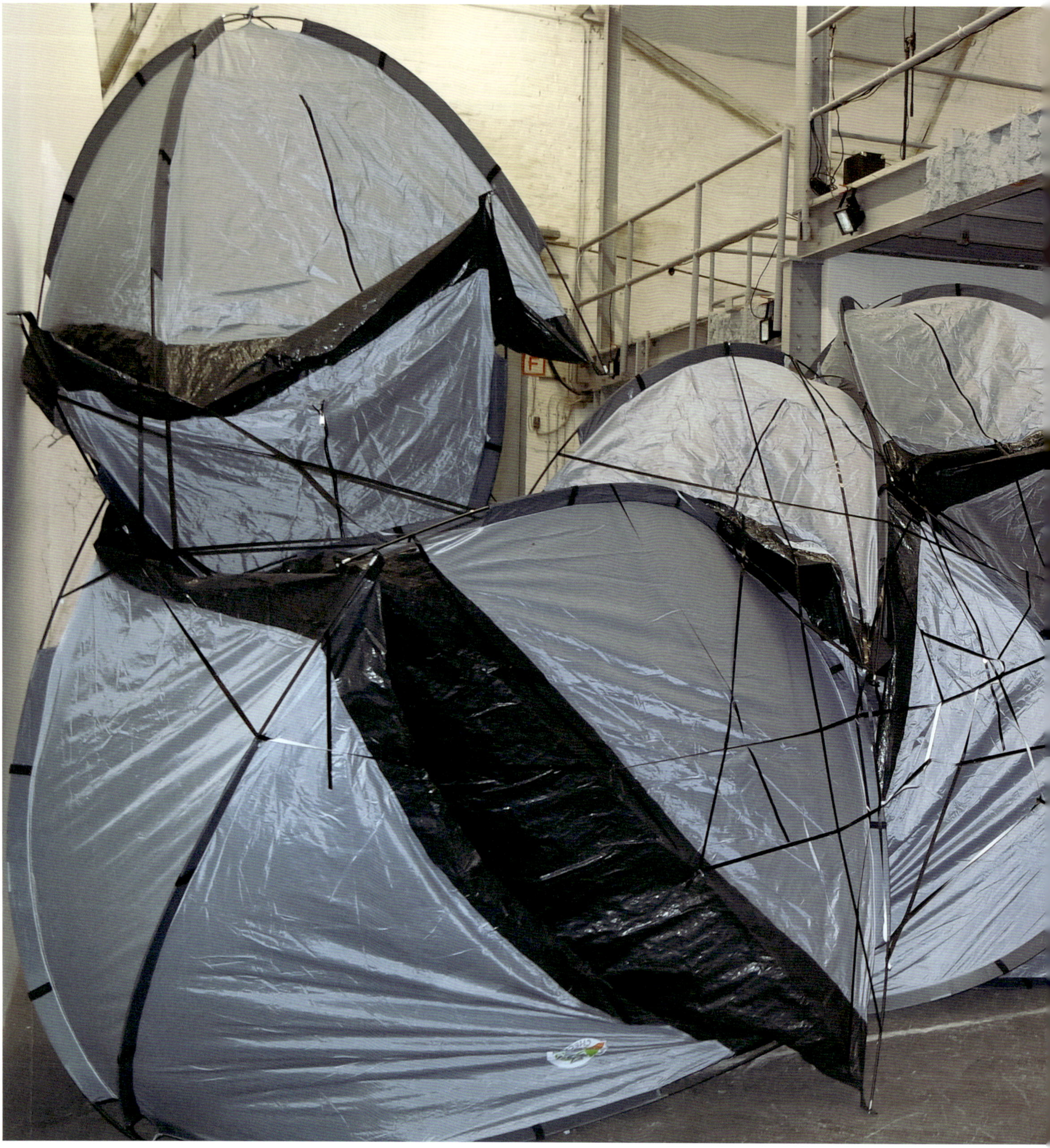

CC4, 2015, tents, adhesive tape, in the background: *Rasta*, 2015, video loop 2 min, colour, without sound, HD 16:9, foil

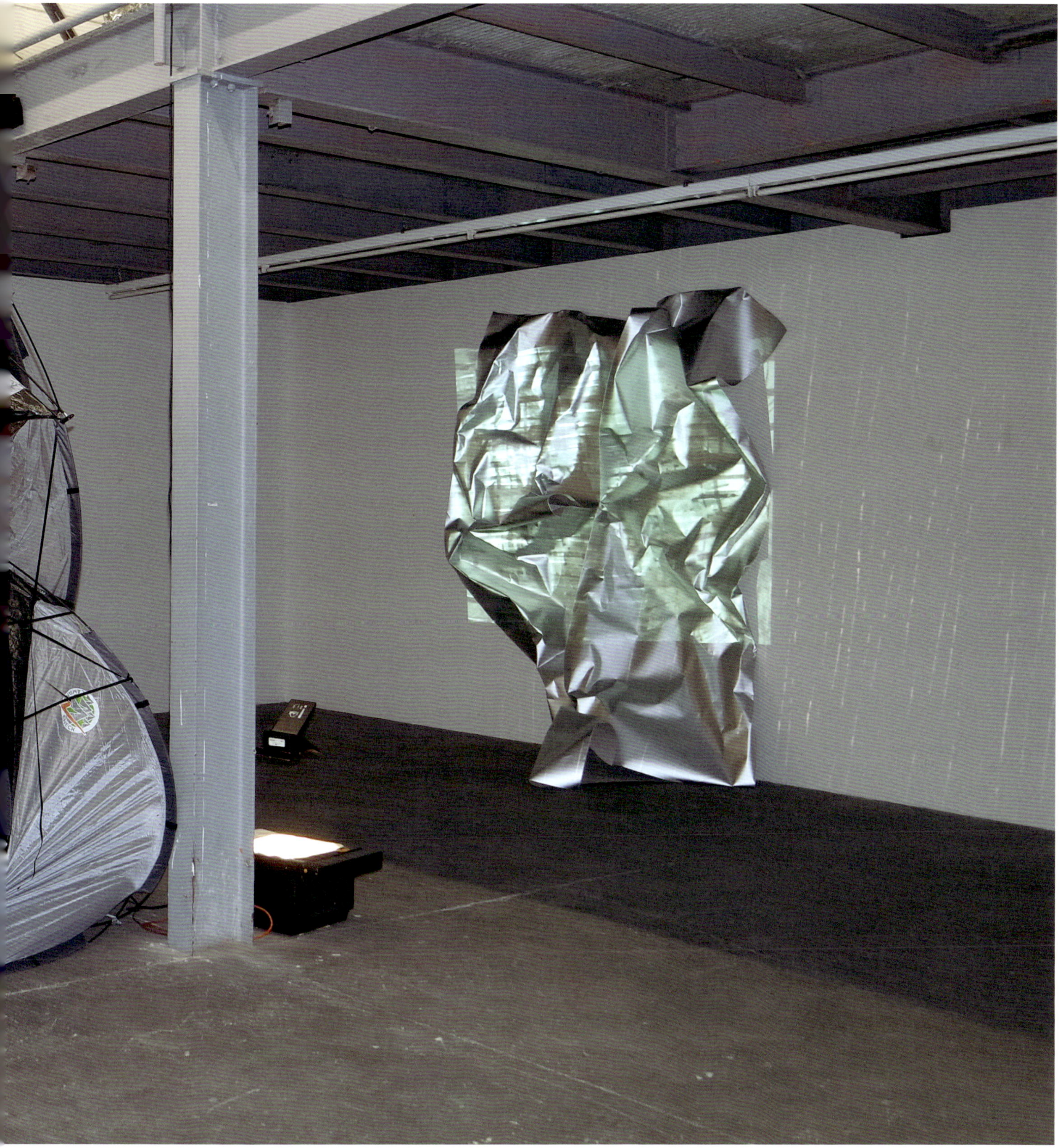

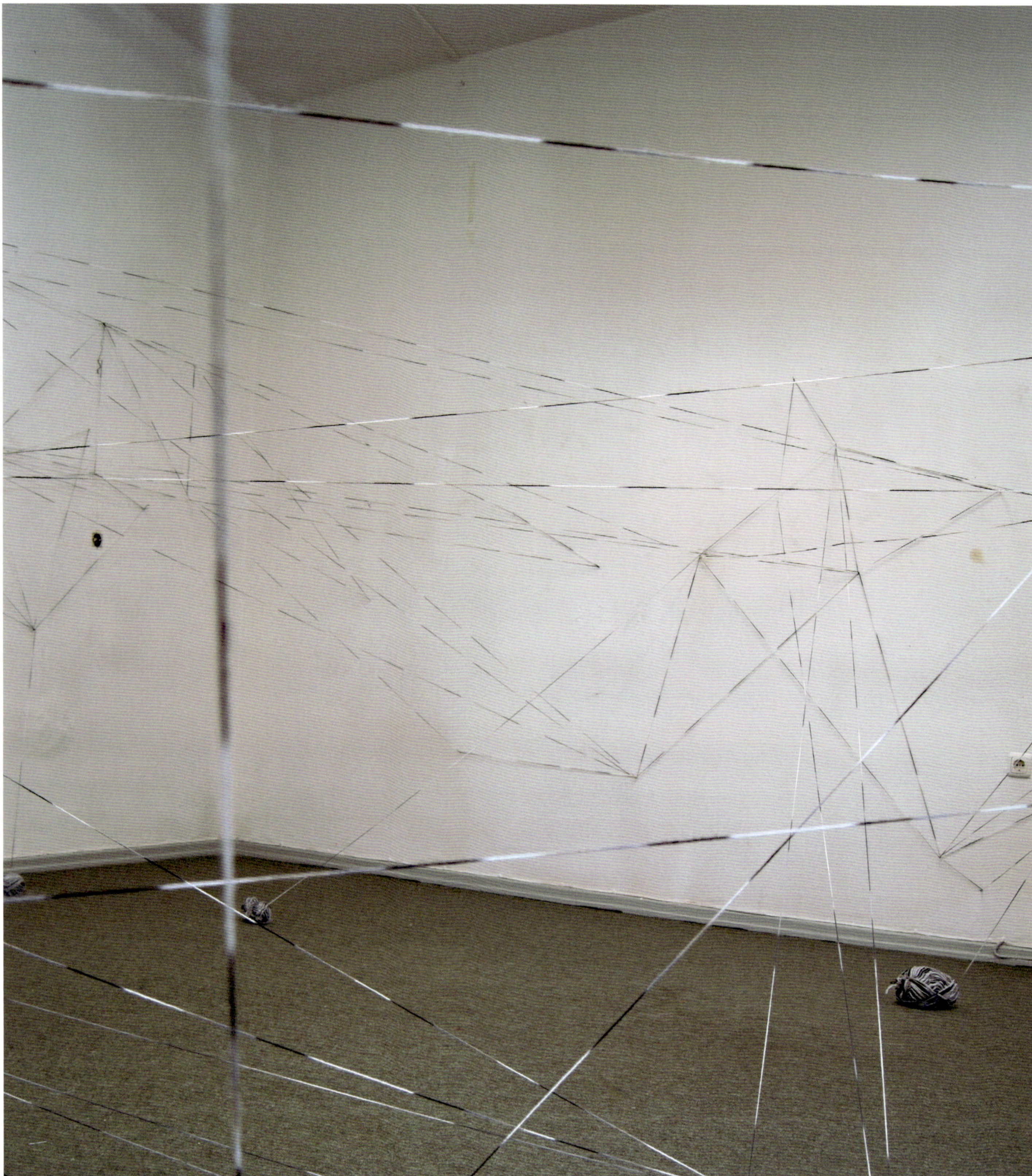

Vorwand FI003, 2017, acrylic wool, space installation

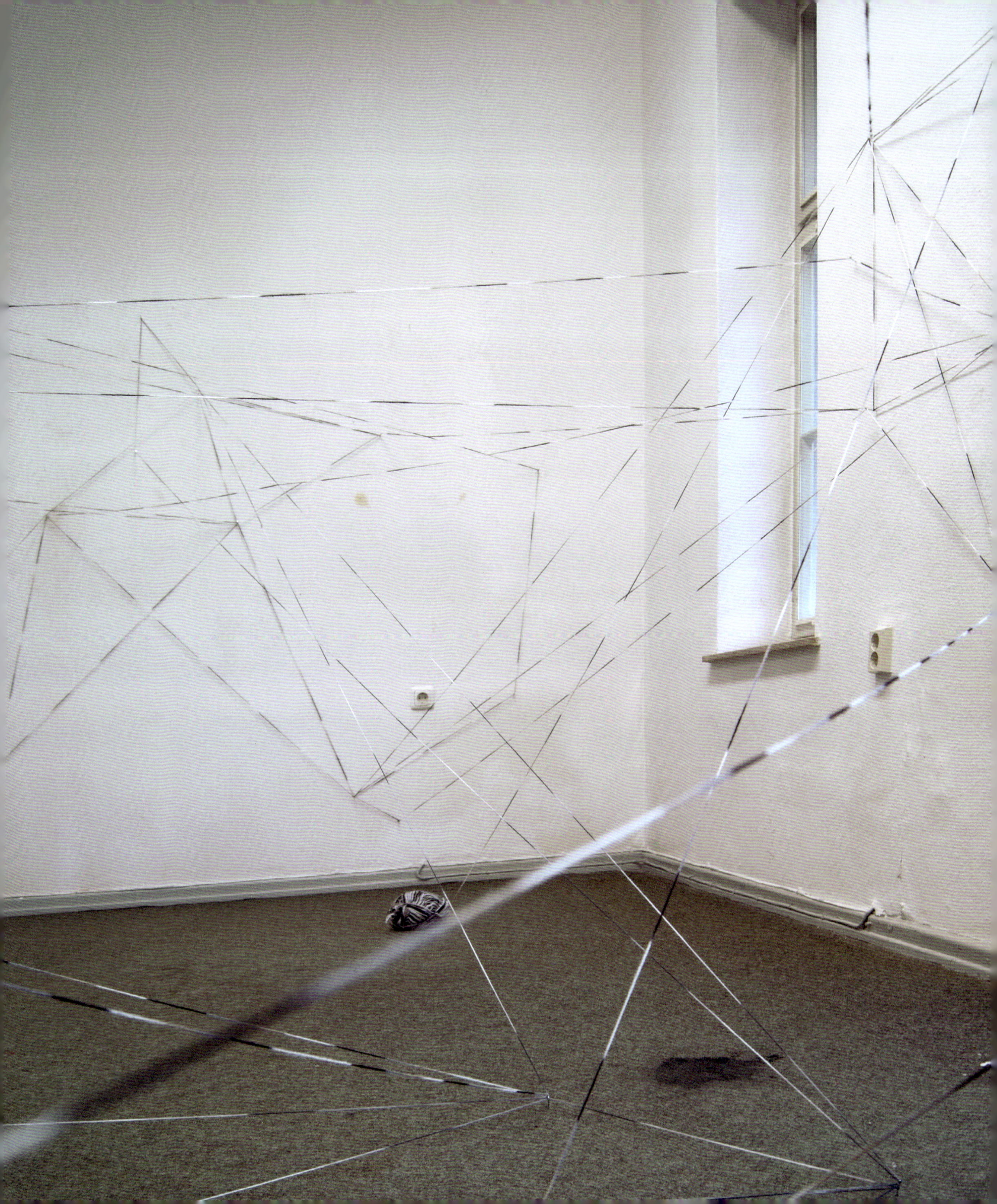

Phi2, 2016, overhead projector, drawing, wire, plaster, 300 x 300 cm

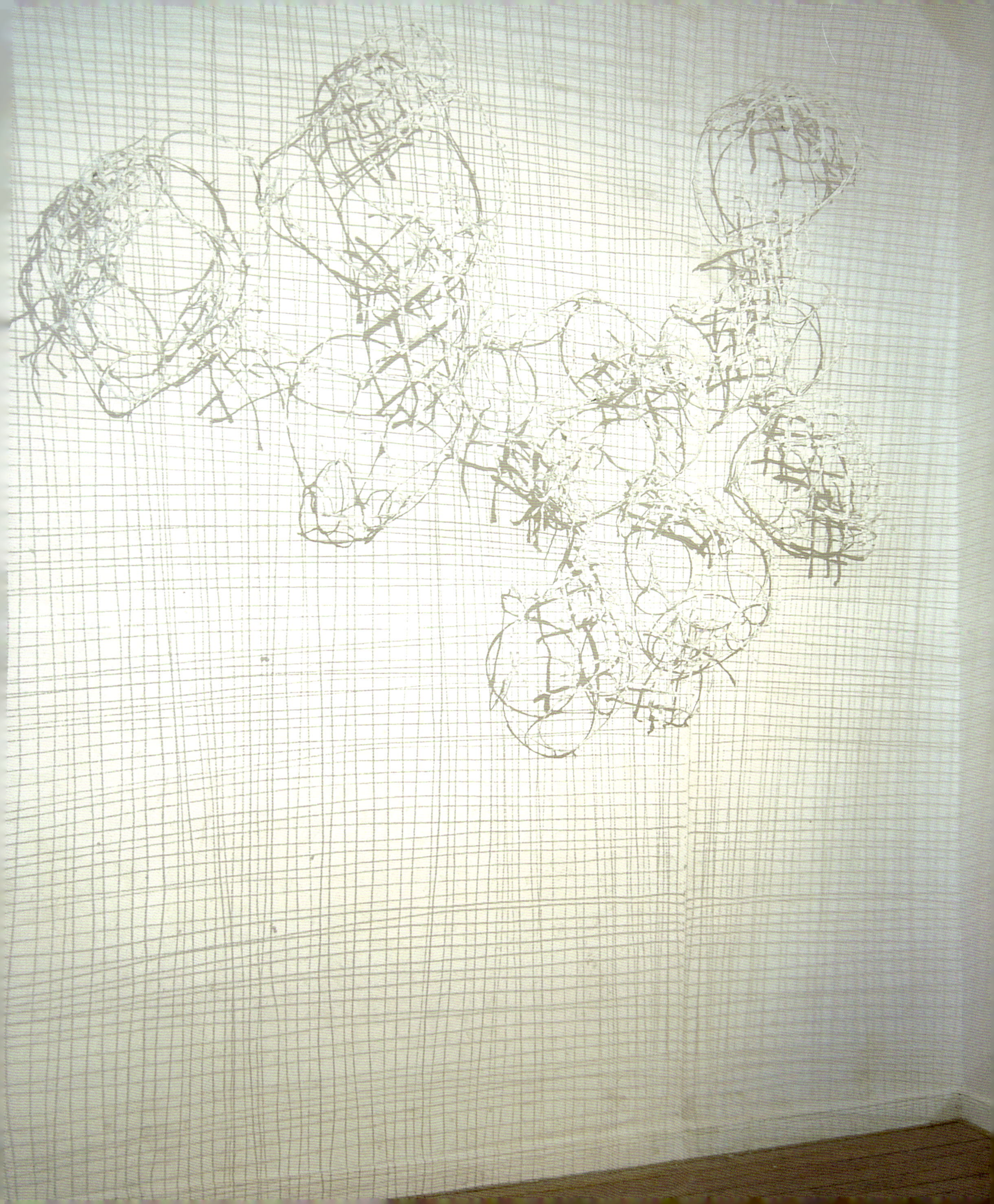

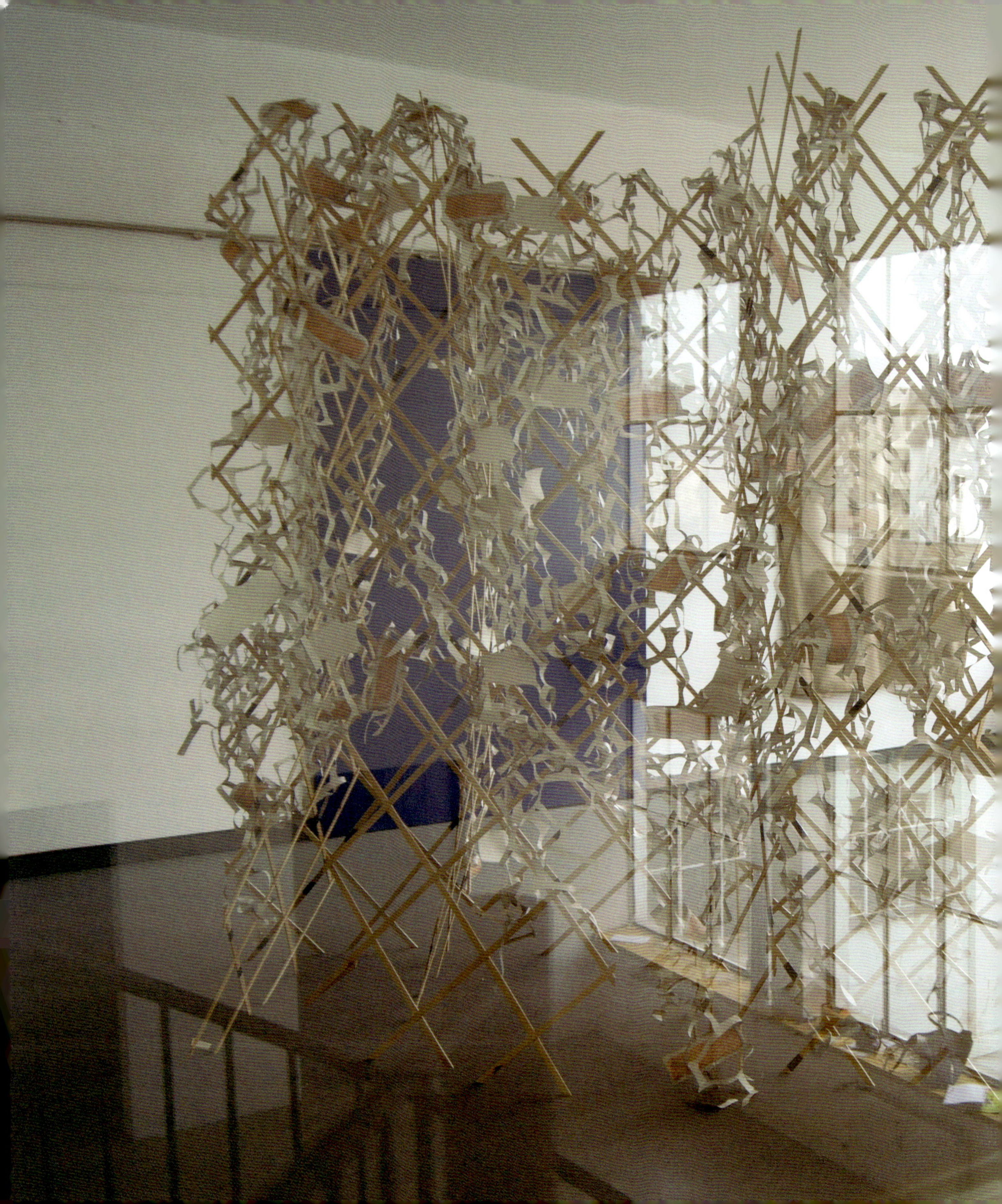

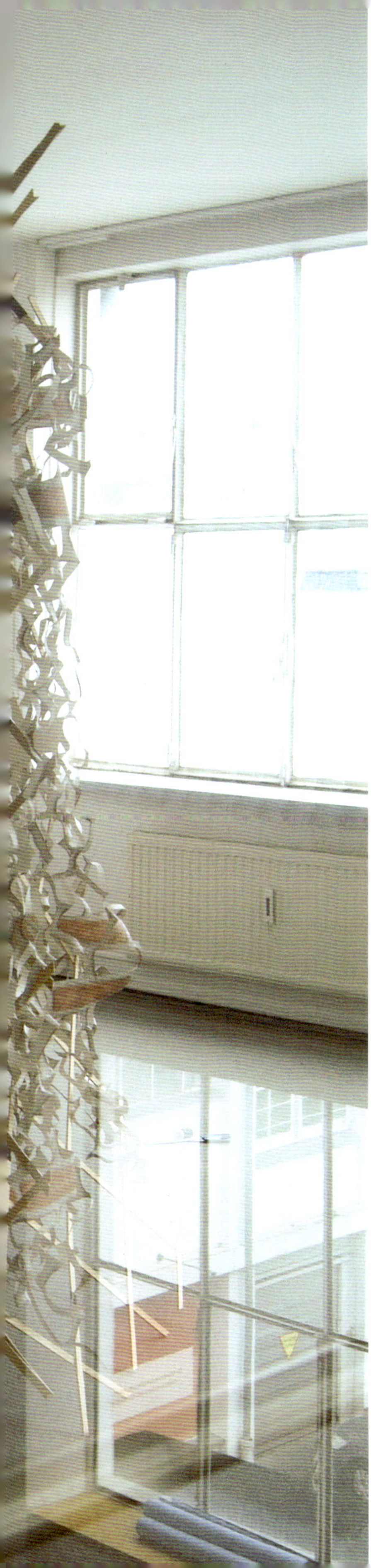

ohNN, 2015, wood, paper wallpaper, dimension variable

Gundi Feyrer
Der Vorhang

Der mit Raum versäumte Blick
flicht sich zu einem Geschehen,
das das Bild ist, das ich sehe,
durchsetzt mit Licht-Punkten
aus Ton und Zeit, die vom Raum
hin- und herbewegt werden.

Ein Vorhang
Sonne scheint Himmel.
Irgendwann hört sie, die Sonne, auf (Vogelgesang), heißt es, auch der Regen. So als wäre nichts geschehen. Da ist nichts geschehen, da geschieht alles, da geschieht nur. Sich verwandelnde Schehen, ein Vorhang wandert in der Sonne, vorwärts getrieben von Luft, Wasser und Regen.

Ein Vorhang hängt im Regen
Alles zusammen ergibt einen Moment, der hängt im Regen, in der Erinnerung, der hängt überall. Aufgehängt im Regen wie die Sonne. Gleich, wann er passierte und geschah, ja, wann geschah es, er? Auf der Fläche eines ganzen Lebens hängt ein Moment, viele, alle Momente. Die Zeit? Welche Zeit? Auch sie, die Zeit, hängt, sitzt, steht überall.
Ich sage morgen, ich sage gestern. Da lief ein Wort an mir vorbei. Es machte Knickse, bellte, fauchte und ließ mich später allein zurück. Mitten in einem vorwärtsgetriebenen Vorhang, der irgendwann von einem Balkon auf die Straße fiel. Zusammen mit dem Moment, in dem er fiel. Zur Seite fiel. Der Vorhang.
Die Momente, Muster in diesem Vorhang, dieser Luft-Tisch-Decke, dem Holzboden, von Raureif bedeckt, auf dem ich in einen Wald Streifen male. Zeichne. Zeichen wirken einen Vorhang, der vollgemalt ist mit Momenten, der vollhängt, vollgehängt ist mit Momenten, die herumstreifen, in einem Vorhang als Vorhang den Boden streifen. Äpfel. Immer wieder.
Alle Himmel wieder blicke ich durch einen neuen Vorhang. Er ist zu lang, er streift am Boden, er hinterlässt Streifen auf dem Holzfußboden, gezeichnet von den Wegen eines leichten Luft-Handschuhs: auf dem Boden.
Ein verbogener Zirkel, den wer, er sich, es, bewegt. Die Erde bewegt die Luft, den Vorhang, die Streifen, die sie im Wald zeichnen, auf die Blätter, die auch gestreift sind. Ich aber bin im Haus und schaue hinaus, auf einen Vorhang hin, den die Sonne bewegt und ihre Wege in meinem Auge herumschickt wie einen Vorhang.
In welcher Zeit, wann geschah das Streifen des Vorhangs auf dem Fußboden?
Er, der Vorhang schaut mir beweglich zu. Ich bewege mich jetzt auf ihn zu. Dann bewegt er sich wieder weg, weg von mir, hinaus auf den Balkon, ergreift die Flucht, faltet sich in ihr, seiner Flucht, auf, bläht sich auf, wird weit und groß und rund. Wann war das?
Die Zeit, die in der Uhr sitzt, schreitet fort: Ich sitze, der Vorhang hängt.
Hier hinaus, auf den Balkon, dort herein. Der Vorhang hat sich aufgebläht und hat geblasen, in meinem Auge, in dem die Zeit sitzt und immer weiter von mir fort: schreitet. Sie entfernt sich von mir, die Zeit, diese, die ich bin und sie mich im Kreis dreht, mir einen Vorhang ins Gesicht bläst. Ich schreite mit ihr fort, in einen Vorhang gehüllt, der sich jetzt wieder in sich selbst eingerollt hat, um in sich selbst fort und weit zu schreiten, um weiter Zeichen zu zeichnen, zu Streifen zu schneiden, ja, das Licht auf dem Fußboden zu meinem Fuß auszuzeichnen.
Mein Fuß ist ganz Fußboden, er kann nicht sein ohne Fußboden, außer er hängt in der Luft wie ein Vorhang, der kürzer ist als der, den ich im Auge habe. Wann war das? Ordne ich die Jahreszahlen richtig ein? Und bringe ich mein Gesicht damit nicht in Unordnung?

Ich stehe auf dem Fuß, auf zwei Füßen, die, wem auch immer gehören. Mir gehören sie nicht; sie gehören zu mir, aber in meinem Besitz sind sie nicht, denn jederzeit kann man sie mir wegneh-

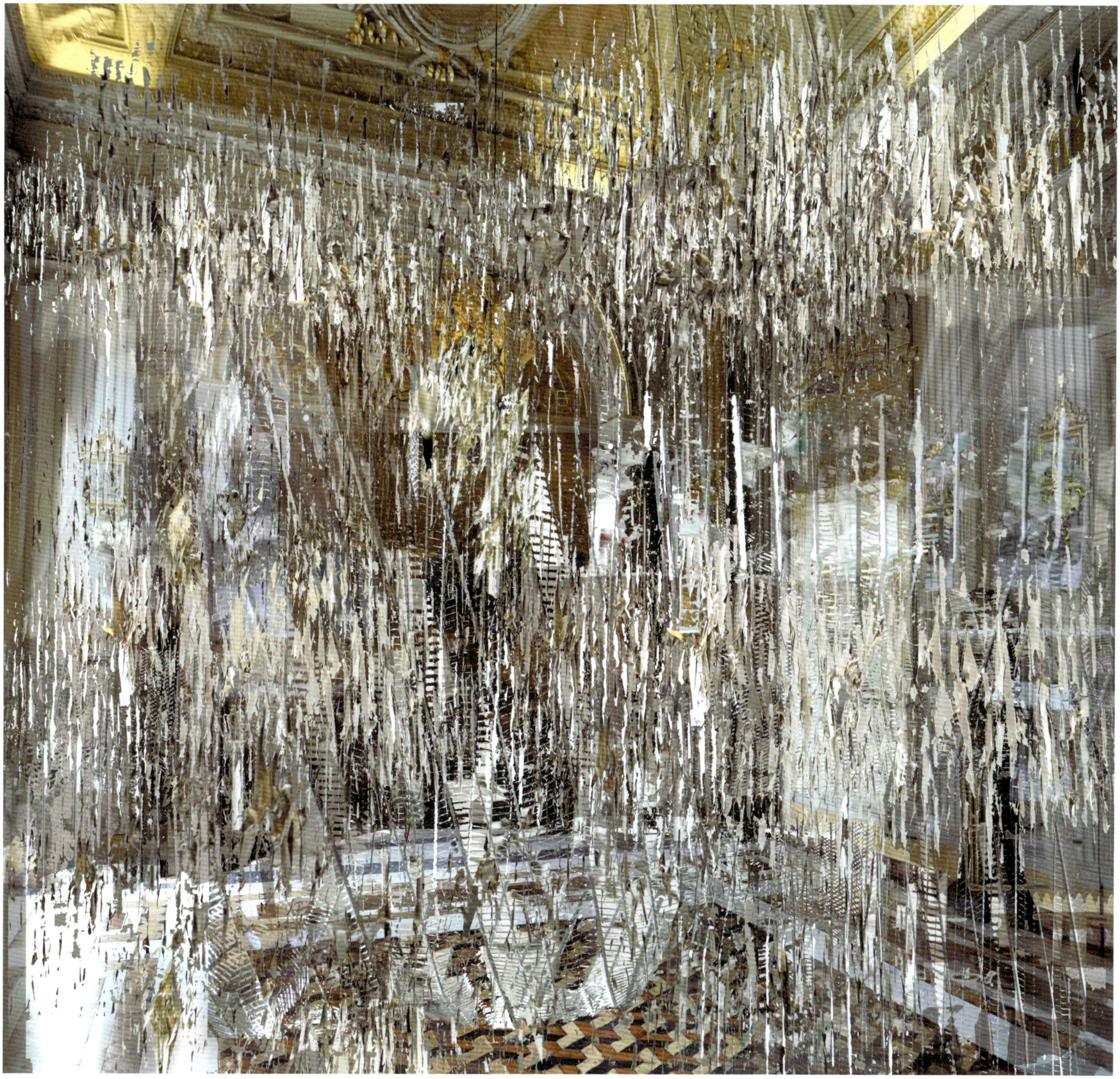

Grossjje4, 2015, photoprint on polyester cloth, 180 x 190 cm

men. Ich ordne die Zeit in die Momente ein, ich ordne die Momente in die Zeit ein. So befand ich mich gestern mitten in einem starken Gewitter: Es tobte. Das Datum seines Tobens habe ich in meinem Kopf festgeschraubt, damit es auf seinen eigenen Füßen stehen kann, damit es in meinem Kopf sicher stehen kann und nicht etwa umfällt, wenn einer kommt und sagt, es sei schon vorgestern gewesen. Da gewesen, dieses starke Gewitter. Eine Basketball-Mannschaft hatte gewonnen und links und rechts wurde auf den Trompeten geblasen, sodass der Vorhang zu zittern begann. Als habe er es nicht gewusst! Kein Anschlag auf die menschliche Freiheit, aber ein Feiertag. Ja, sind sie denn alle verrückt geworden?
Der Vorhang bleibt und so wie er immer bleibt in seinem Bleiben, das ein stetes Wandern ist, vorwärtsgetrieben von Luft, Licht und Wasser, unterbrochen durch ein ab und zu Im-Regen-Hängenbleiben. Dann hängt er zwar seltsamerweise gar nicht, sondern verdrückt sich schlapp in einer Ecke, schleift, von etwaigem Wind getrieben, auf dem Boden hin und her.

Später surrte die Arbeit auf der Straße unten um ihn herum und die Tage wurden immer noch länger. Auch der Vorhang sah so, nassgeworden, länger aus als sonst. Ich saß an einem Tisch und blickte an ihm vorbei, als gäbe es ihn gar nicht, ihn, den vom Regen nass- und schmutzig gewordenen Vorhang, der sich jetzt kaum mehr bewegte und auch nicht mehr hing. Er hatte den Boden berührt, ja, meinen mir ganz eigenen Fußboden, an den er sich jetzt zu klammern schien, ja, es sah aus, als ob er an ihm klebte.

Später und an einem ganz anderen und sehr trockenen Tag saß ich an einem bunten und mit lustigen Farben gefüllten Tisch, mit einem sich im Wind drehenden Vorhang hinter mir, der mich ab und zu berührte. Ich weiß nicht mehr, wann es war. Er berührte mich wenig, vielleicht zehnmal in der Stunde und erinnerte mich an die Drehung der Erde.

Einige Male hatte mich der Vorhang daran gehindert, umzufallen, hatte er mich mit seinem Hängen vorwärtsgeschoben, in den Tag hinein. Wann genau das war, weiß ich nicht mehr, ich könnte es jetzt nicht mehr einfach sagen.

Der Morgen taut auf, fällt mir ins Gesicht. Dann habe ich ihn im Gesicht. Dann ist mein Gesicht der Spiegel des Morgens. Dann ist mein Gesicht selbst aus ihm, dem Morgen gemacht, ist selbst dieser eine Morgen, der mir vorhin auf einmal ins Gesicht gefallen ist und immer noch, den ganzen Morgen lang, mir dort, im Gesicht, immer anders hängenbleibt. Dann atme ich ihn, ihn, den Morgen, hole Luft aus ihm heraus, aus ihm, der ich selber bin. Und immer anders. Und der mir vorhin ins Gesicht gefallen ist. Mit einem Mal und immer anders.

Später geht er weg, er, der Morgen,
und löst sich auf, in meinem Gesicht,
beginnt, irgendwo zu schwimmen.
Noch später fielen die Vögel aus dem Tag heraus.

Gundi Feyrer

The Curtain

The eye, entangled in space,
forms into an event,
it is the picture I see,
pierced by holes of light,
sound and time,
which are moved back and forth:
by space, by a curtain.

A Curtain
Sun shines heavens.
Sometime he, the sun, stops (birdsong), so they say, also the rain. Stops. As if nothing had happened. Nothing did happen, everything is happening, there is nothing but happening. Changing events, a curtain wanders in the sun, driven forward by air, water and rain.

A Curtain Is Hanging in the Rain
Everything together creates a moment, which hangs in the rain, hangs in reminiscence, hangs everywhere. Hung up in the rain just like the sun. Is hung up in heaven. No matter when the moment happened and chanced, so yes, when did it chance? It, the moment? Hung up on the surface of an entire life, there is hung up one moment, some, all moments. Time? Which time? Time, too, is hanging, sitting, standing everywhere.

I say tomorrow, I say yesterday. There was a word passing me by. It dropped a curtsey, barked, hissed and left me behind, later. In the middle of a forward pushed-forward curtain which fell down from a balcony onto the street. Sometime. Together with the moment in which it fell. To the side. The curtain.
The moments, patterns in this curtain, in this air-table-cloth, this wooden floor covered with frost, on which I paint stripes, converting them into a forest. I'm drawing. Signs effect a curtain, getting fulfilled with painted moments, in a curtain full of moments striping around and brushing and touching the floor in a curtain as a curtain.
Apples. Again and again.

Every heaven again I look through a new curtain. It is too long, it brushes the ground, it leaves behind stripes on the wooden floor, drawn by the paths of a light air-glove: on the floor.
A bent circle moved by whom, him, it, itself moves. The earth moves the air, the curtain, the stripes they draw in the forest onto leaves and striped papers. But I am inside the house, looking outside, at a curtain, moved by the sun and sending his directions around and into my eye like a curtain.
In which time, so, when did the brushing of the curtain on the floor happen?

It, the curtain, is watching me while it moves. Now I move towards it. Then it moves again, away from me, out and onto the balcony, it takes to flight, folding itself into its flight, yeah, it blows up, it becomes wide and big and round.
When did that happen?

Time is sitting inside the clock, pacing forward: I sit, the curtain hangs.
Out here, onto the balcony, inside there. The curtain has blown up and it is blowing, in the middle of my eye, this place in which time is sitting, while stepping forward. It's moving away from me, it, this time which is me. It spins me around, blowing a curtain into my face. I step forward together with it, time, covered in a curtain which now rolls itself back into itself, in order to step forward, moving on, drawing on, signing signs, cutting stripes, drawing light on the floor, creating my foot.
My foot is floor, it cannot be without floor, unless it hangs in the air like a curtain, shorter than the one sitting in my eye. When did that happen? Do I arrange the years correctly? And won't I throw my own face into disorder?

I'm standing on my foot, on two feet that belong to whomever. They do not belong to me; they belong to me, but they are not in my posses-

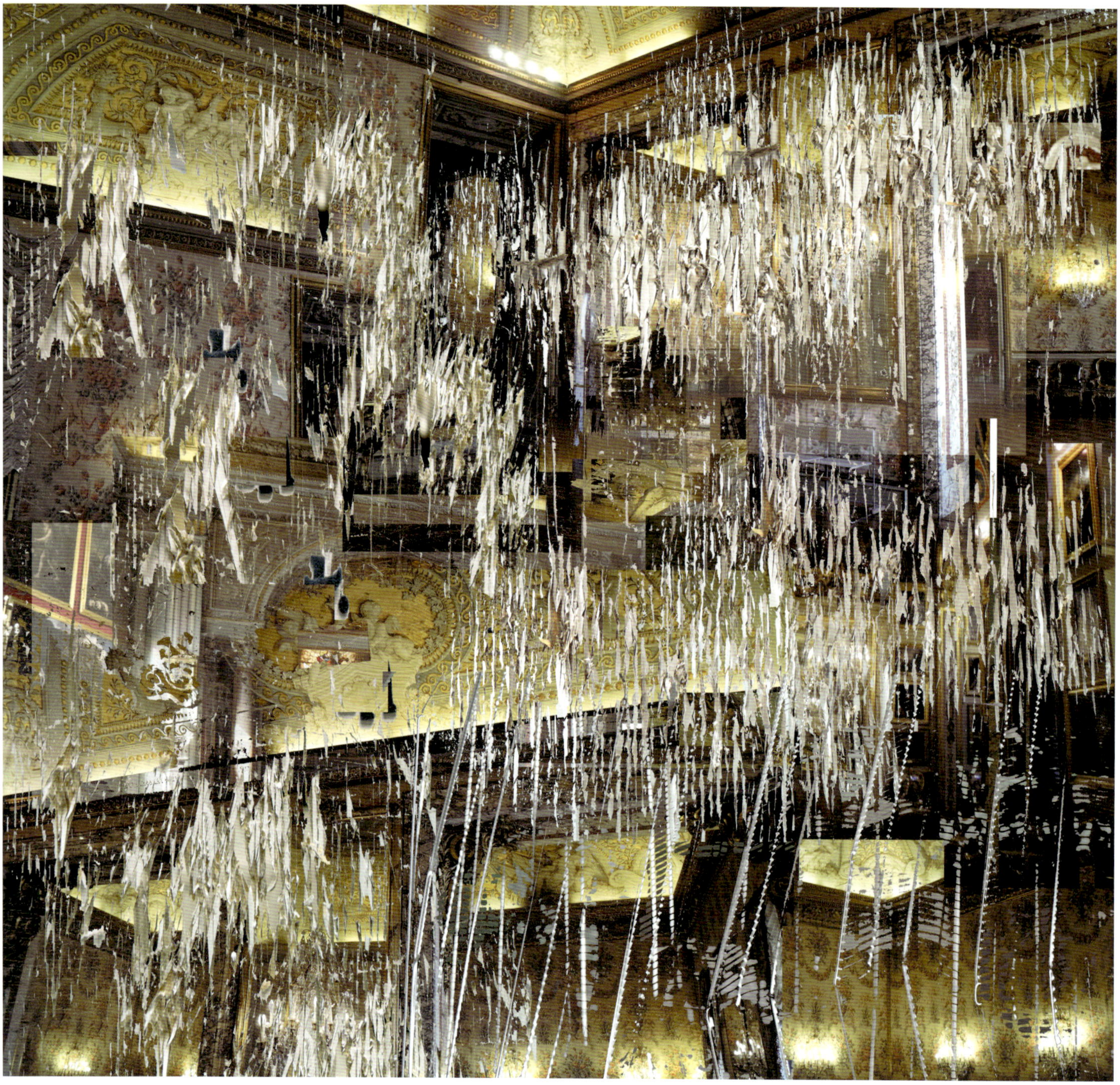

Grossko, 2015, photoprint on polyester cloth, 180 x 190 cm

sion, for they can be taken away from me at any time. I arrange time in the order of the moments, I arrange moments in the order of time. So yesterday I found myself in the middle of a heavy thunderstorm: it raged. I screwed the date of its raging into my head so that it can stand on its own feet, so that it can stand securely in my head without tottering, if someone were to come and say that it happened the day before yesterday. The heavy thunderstorm happened. A basketball team had won and to left and right they blew on the trumpets, so the curtain began to tremble. As if it hadn't known yet! No attack on human freedom, but a holiday. Are they all out of their minds?
The curtain remains and remains as it always has in its stay, which is a constant wandering, propelled forward by air, light and water, interrupted by an occasional rain-clogging. Then, strangely enough, it doesn't hang at all, but rather slouches limply in a corner, drags itself back and forth over the ground, driven by some air.

Later, work buzzed down in the street, around the curtain, and days became even longer. Also the curtain looked like this, got wet, longer than usual. I sat at a table and looked past it as if it didn't exist at all, it, the curtain, which had become wet and dirty from the rain, which now hardly moved and no longer hung. It had touched the floor, my very own floor, to which it now seemed to cling, yes, it looked as if it was glued to it.

Later and on a completely different and very dry day, I sat at a colourful table filled with cheerful colours, with a curtain behind me spinning in the wind, which touched me from time to time. I can't remember when it was. It touched me rarely, maybe ten times an hour and reminded me of the rotation of the earth.

Several times the curtain had prevented me from falling over, it had pushed me forward with its hanging, into the day. I can't remember exactly when that was, I simply couldn't say it now.

Morning thaws, falls into my face. Then I have it right in my face. Then my face is the mirror of the morning. Then my face itself is made out of it, the morning, even is that one morning, which suddenly fell into my face earlier and still, all morning long, remaining there for me, in my face, always different. Then I breathe it, it, the morning, I take air out of it, out of it who is me. And always different. And who fell into my face earlier. All at once and always different.

Later it goes away, it, the morning,
dissolves in my face,
starts swimming somewhere.
Even later, the birds fell out of the day.

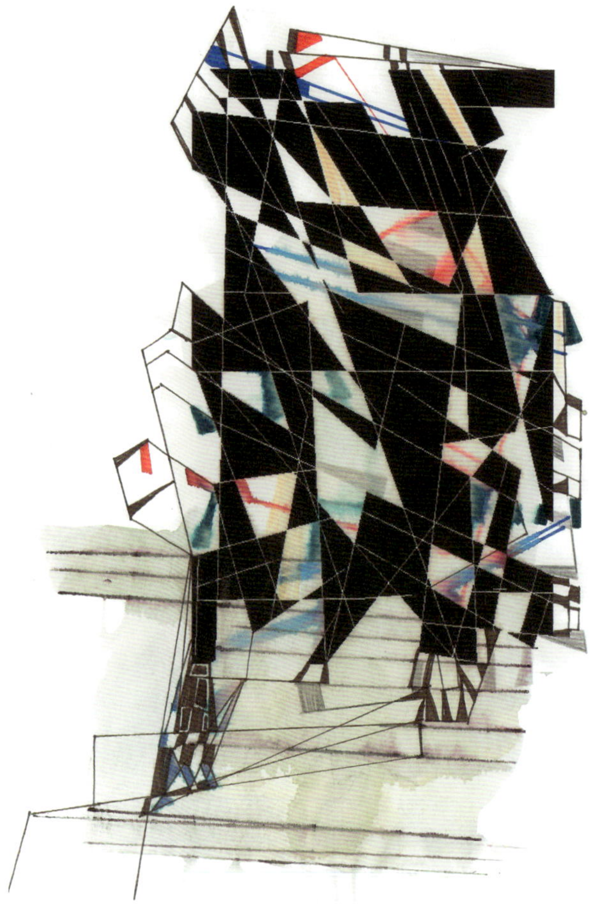

EF1, 2014, water colour, coloured pencil, pigment liner on digital drawing, 29.7 x 21 cm

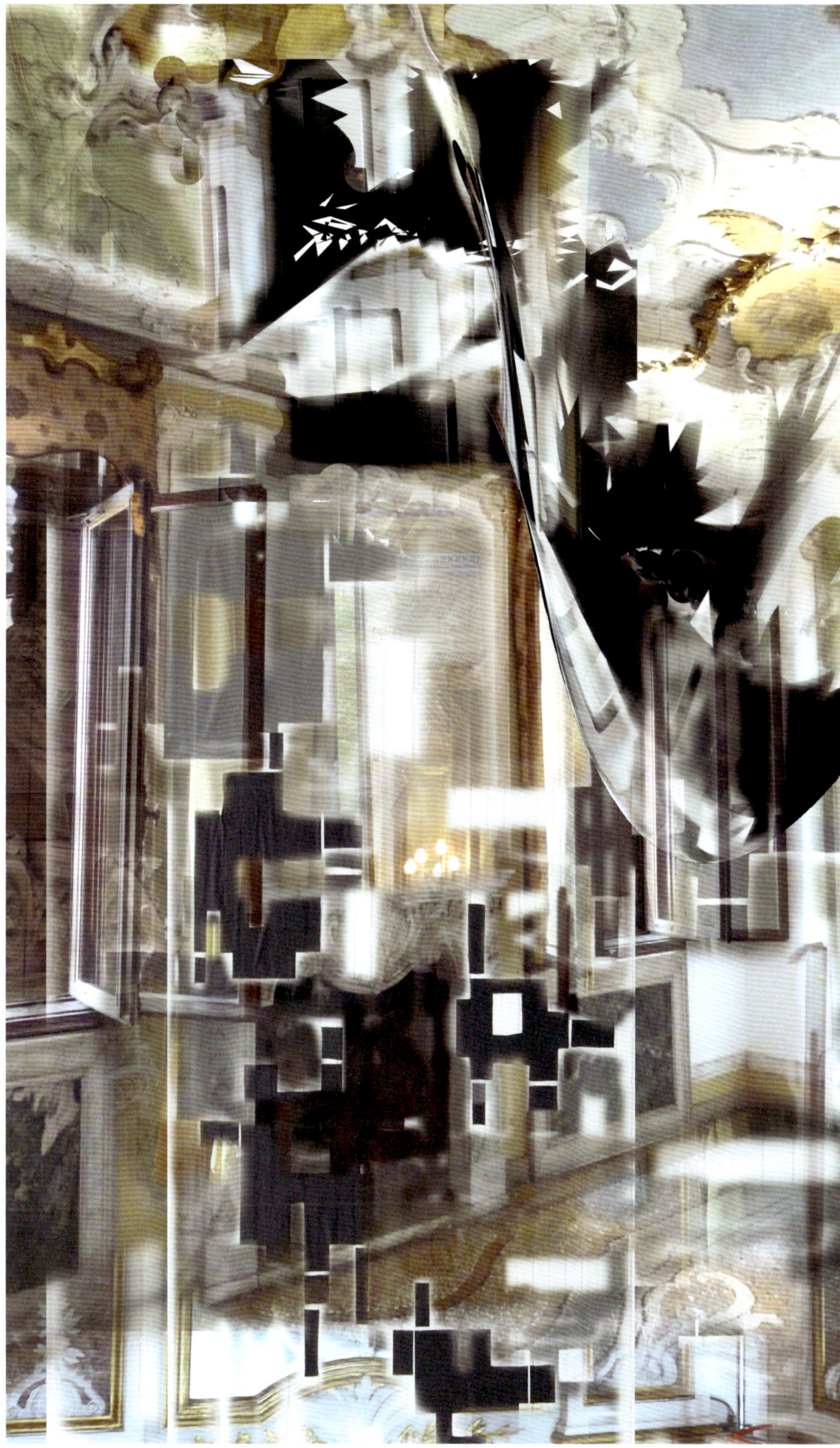

textebi-finis, 2012, photoprint on polyester cloth, 220 x 130 cm

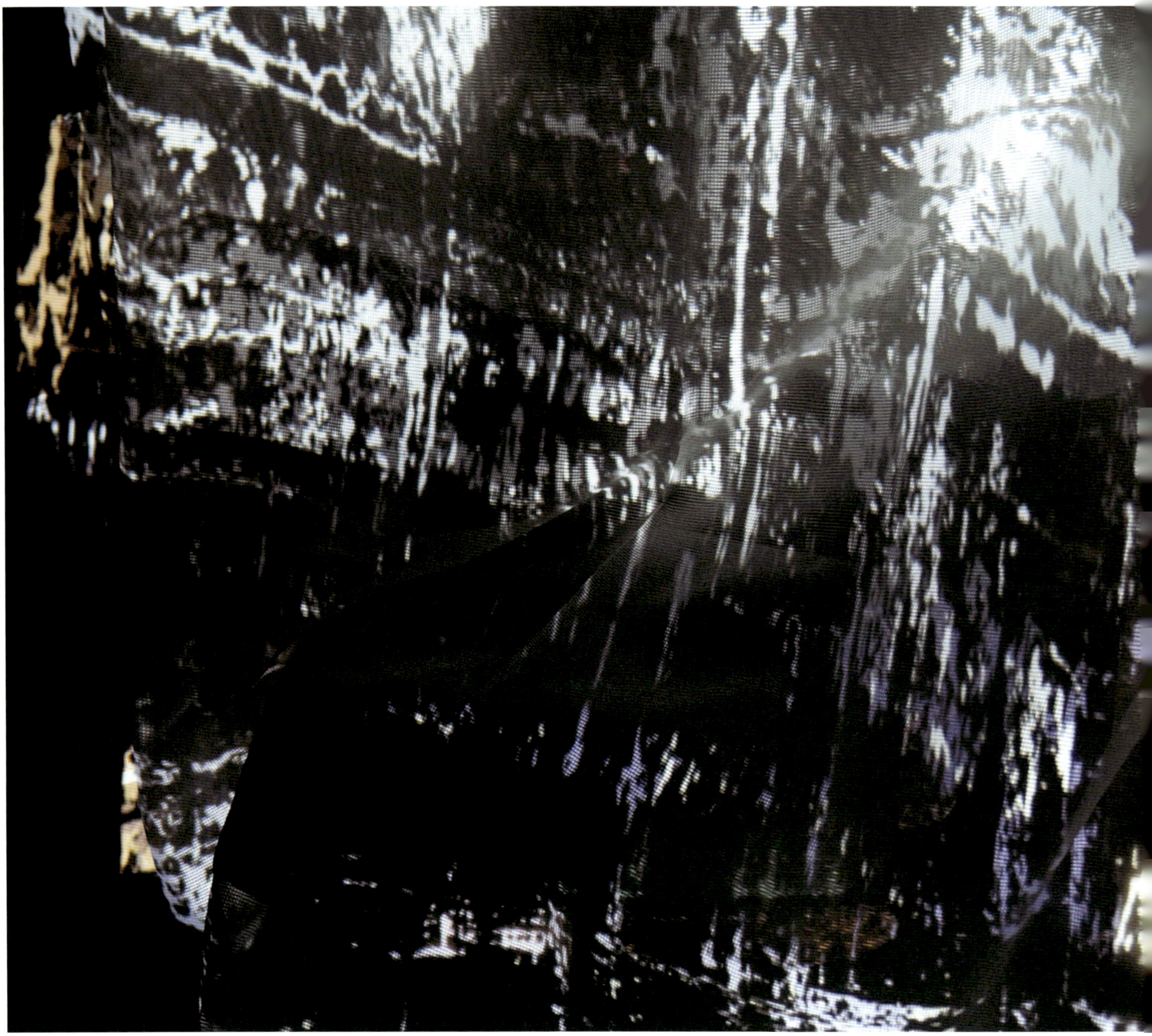

arist, 2014, photoprint on polyester cloth, 80 x 200 cm

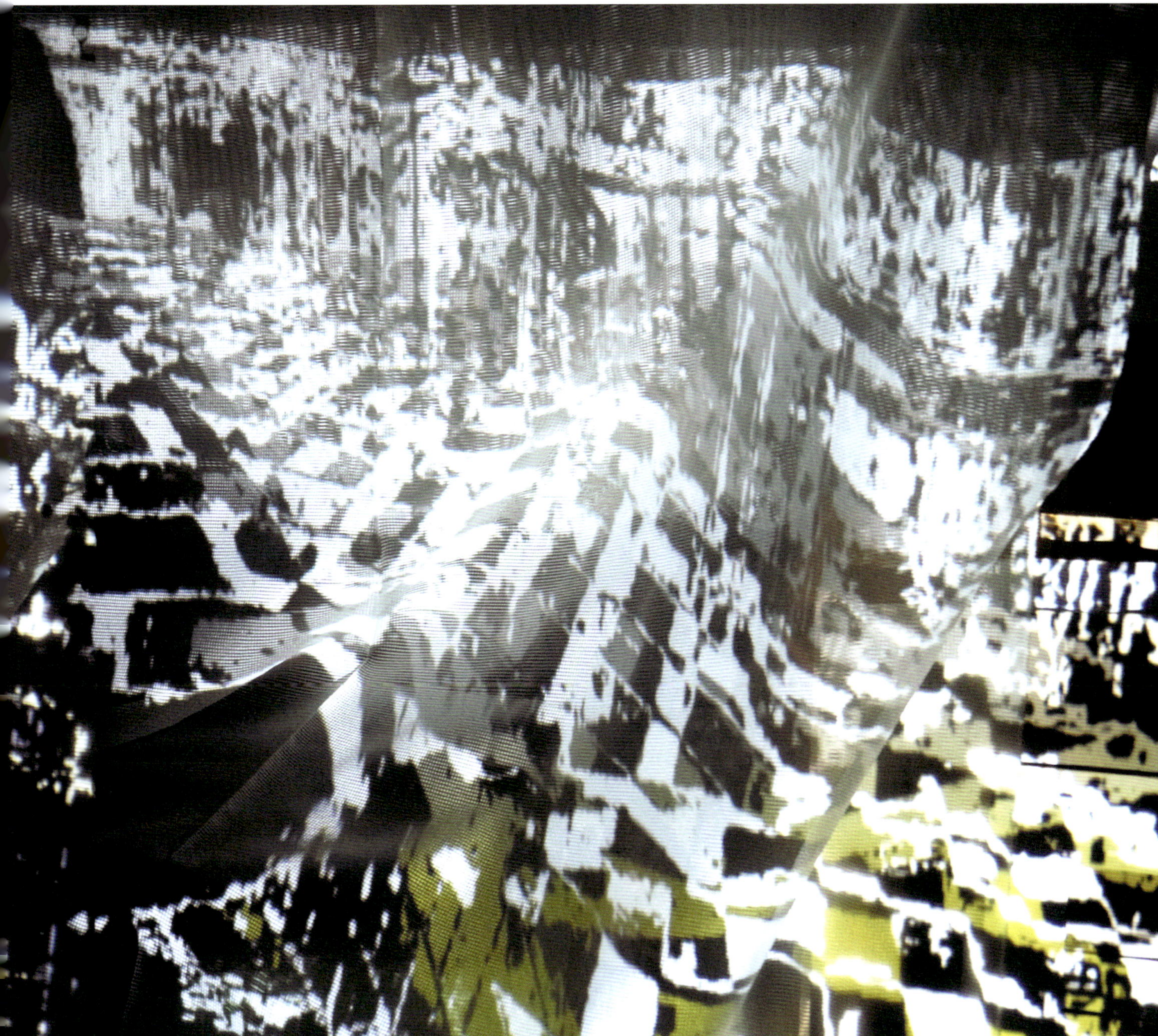

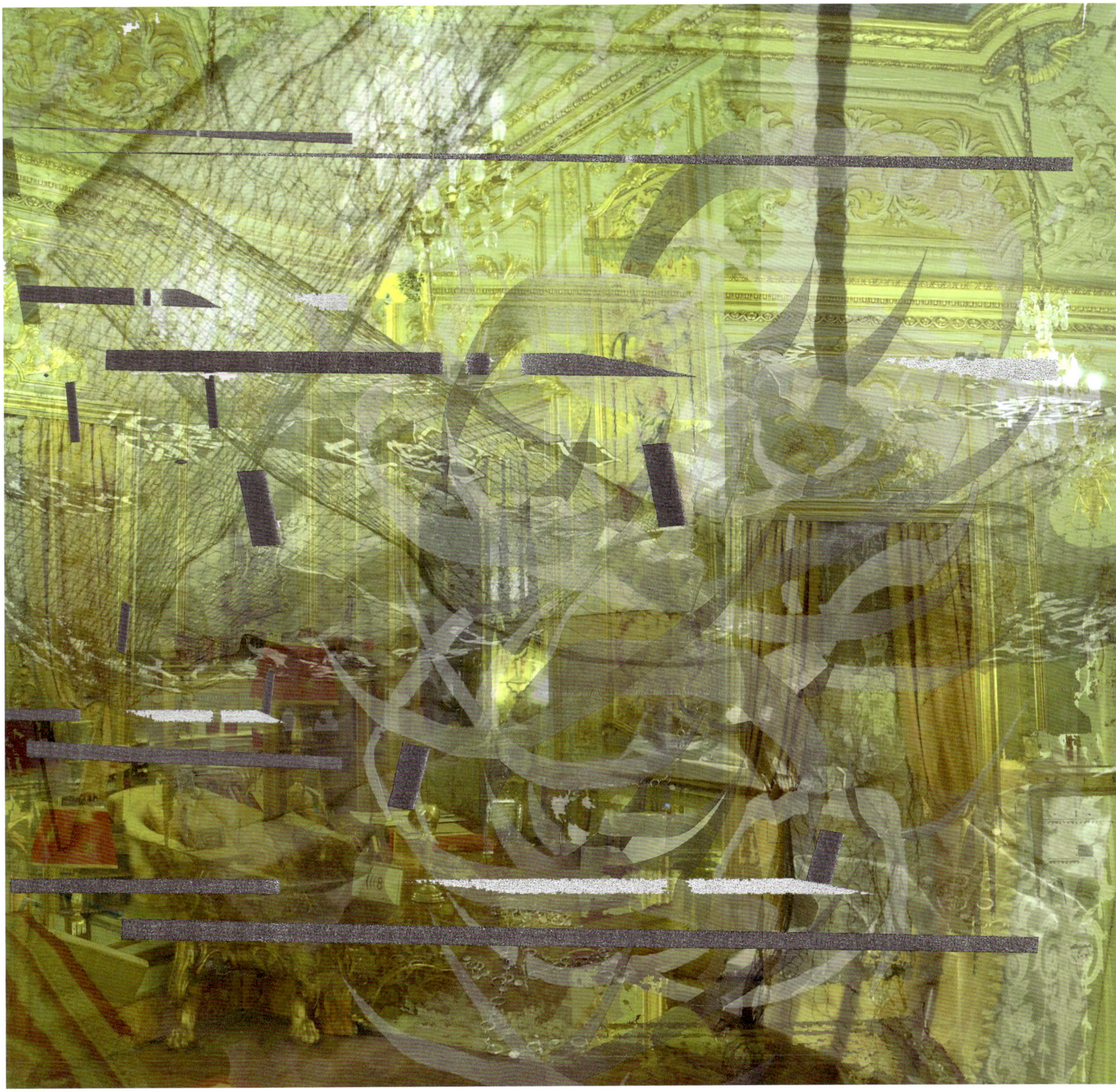

gross6b, 2015, photoprint on polyester cloth, 180 x 190 cm

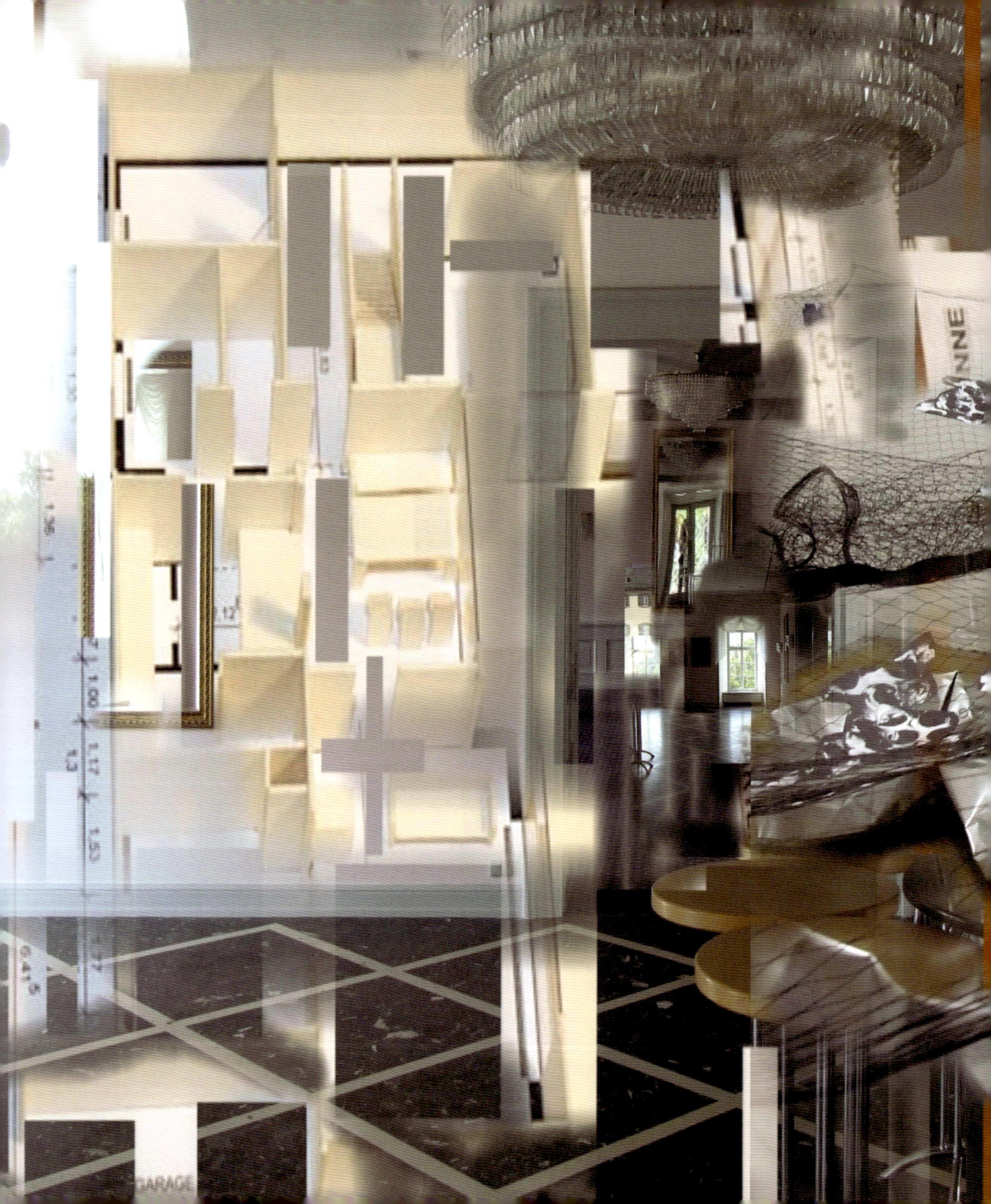
GARAGE

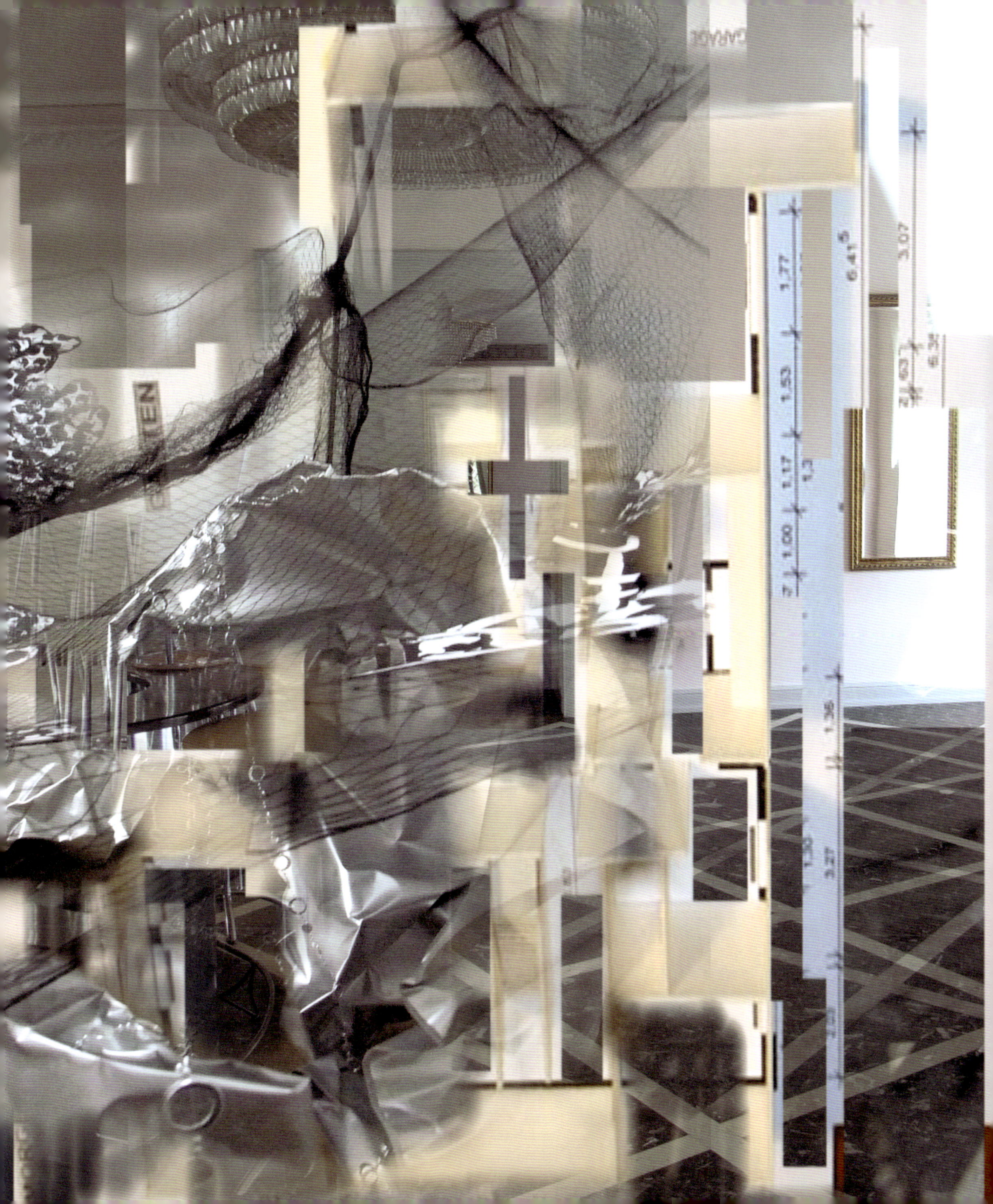

Previous page: *hom1*, 2012, photoprint on polyester cloth, 130 x 210 cm

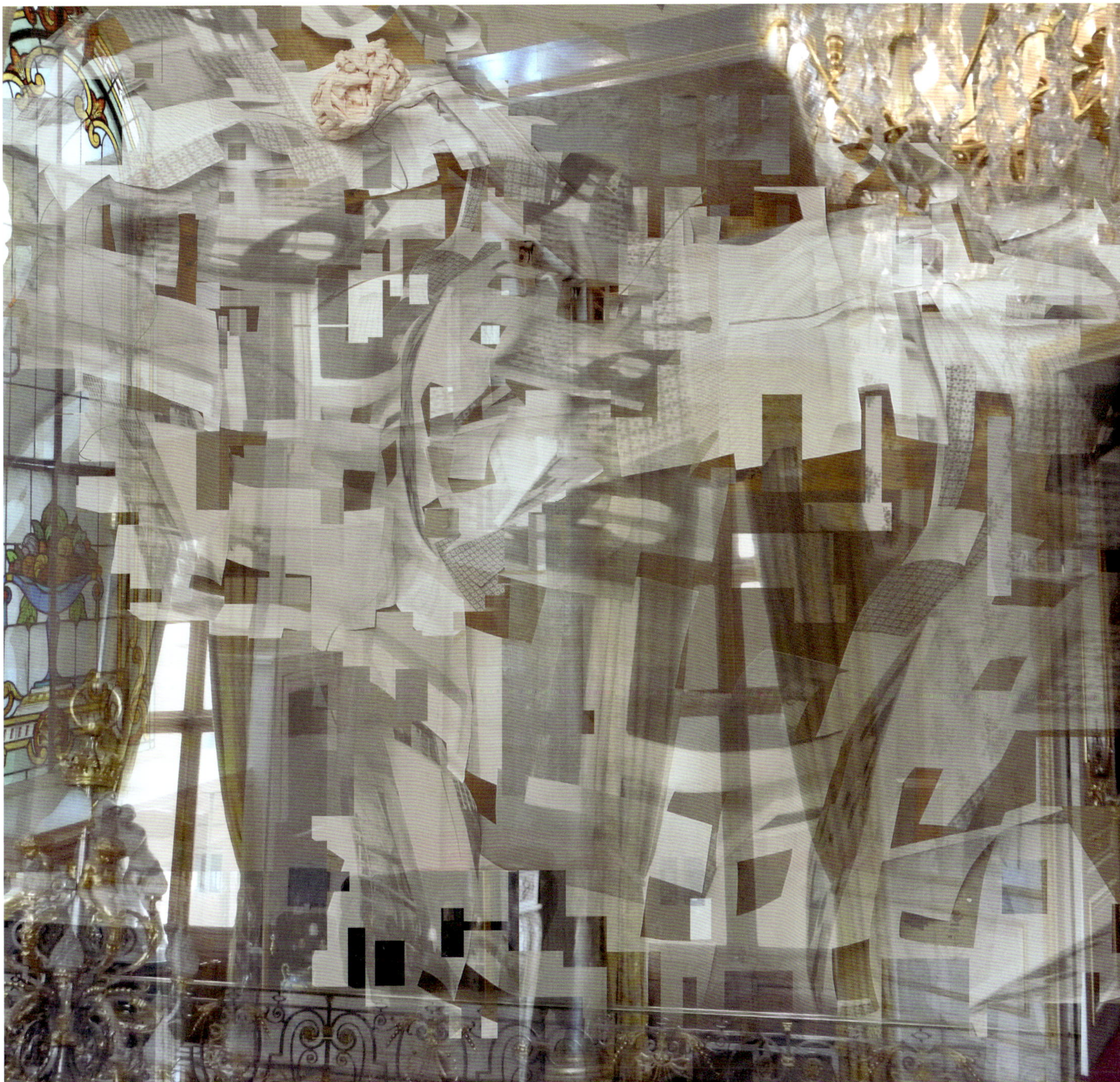

Rump-I 1b, 2015, photoprint on polyester cloth, 180 x 190 cm

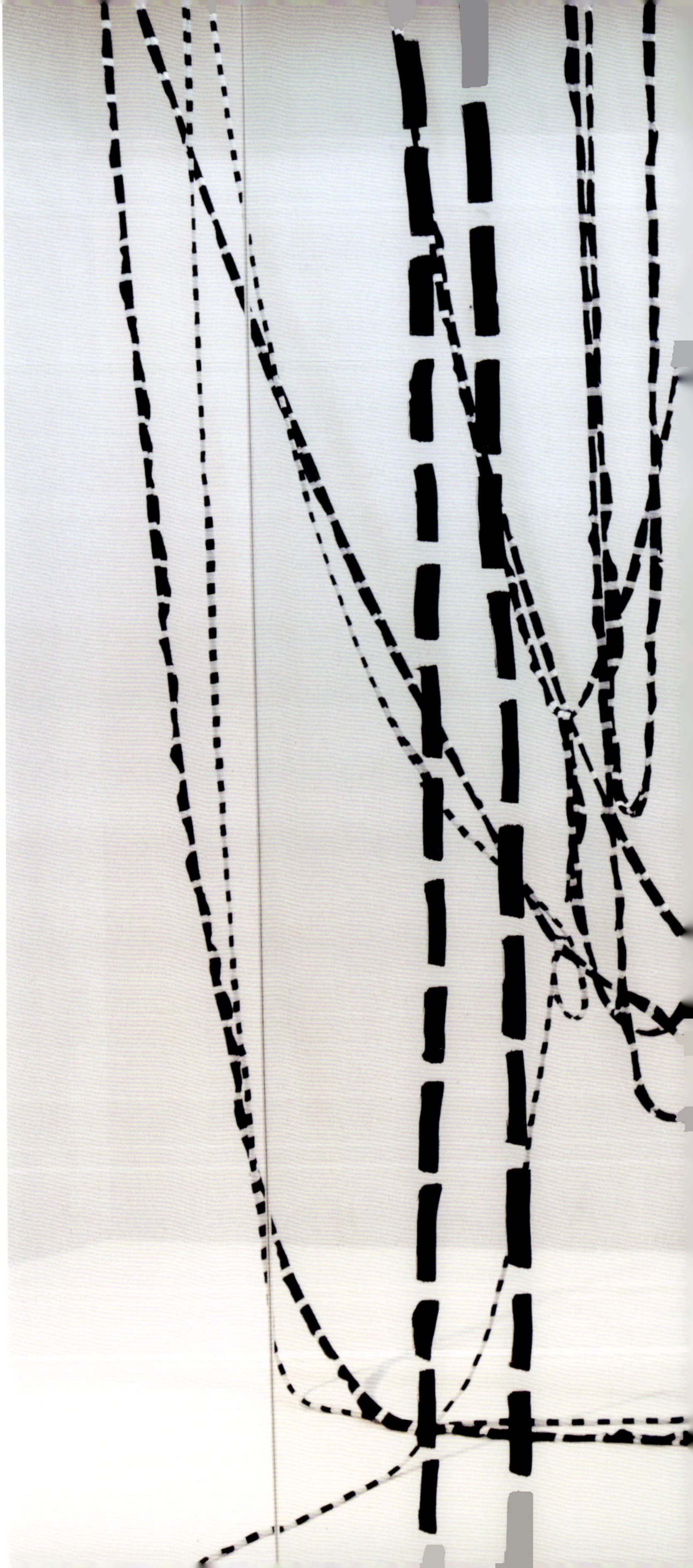

Hub nach Richtung 4, 2019, glass cabinet, chalk, yarn, dimension variable

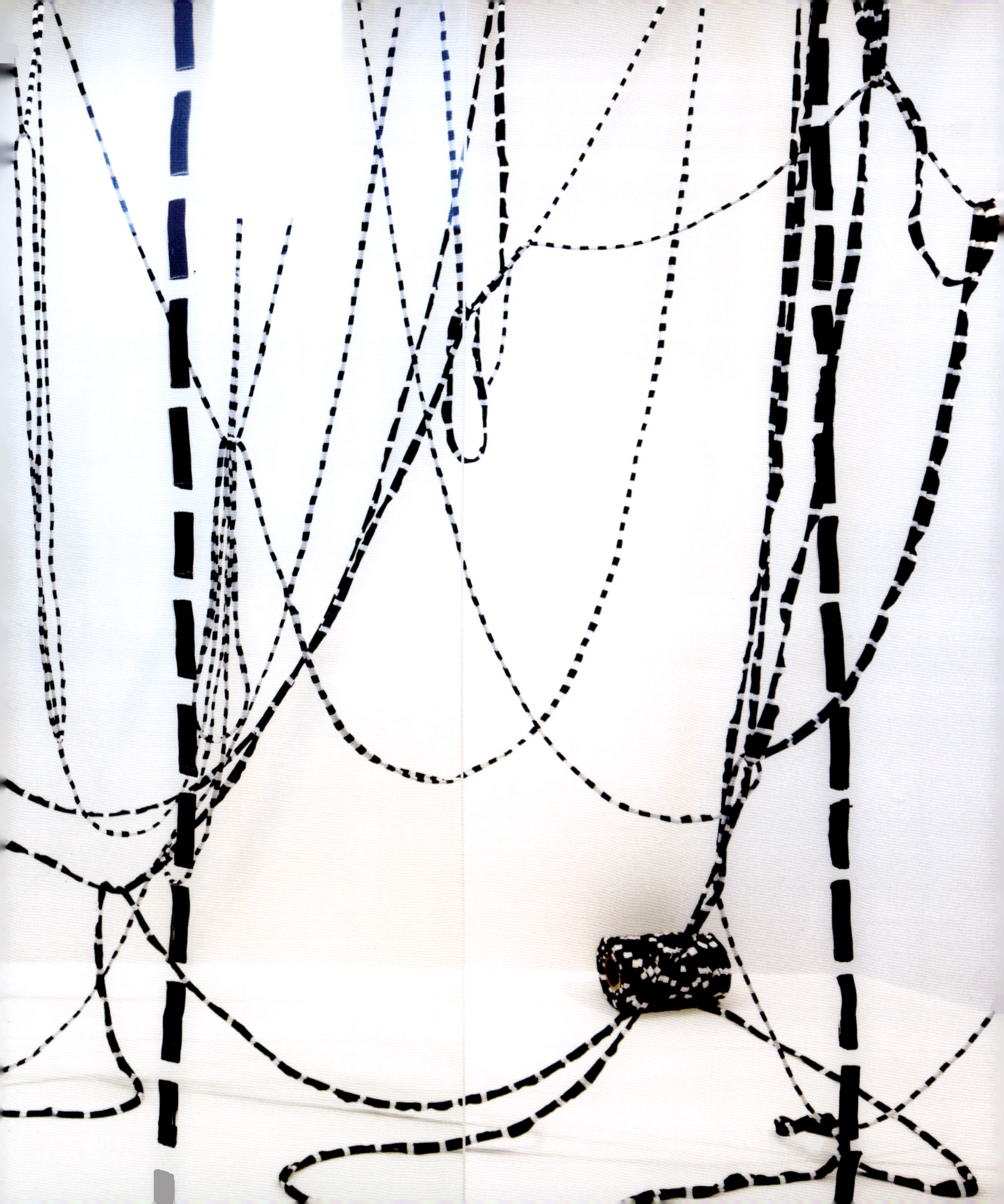

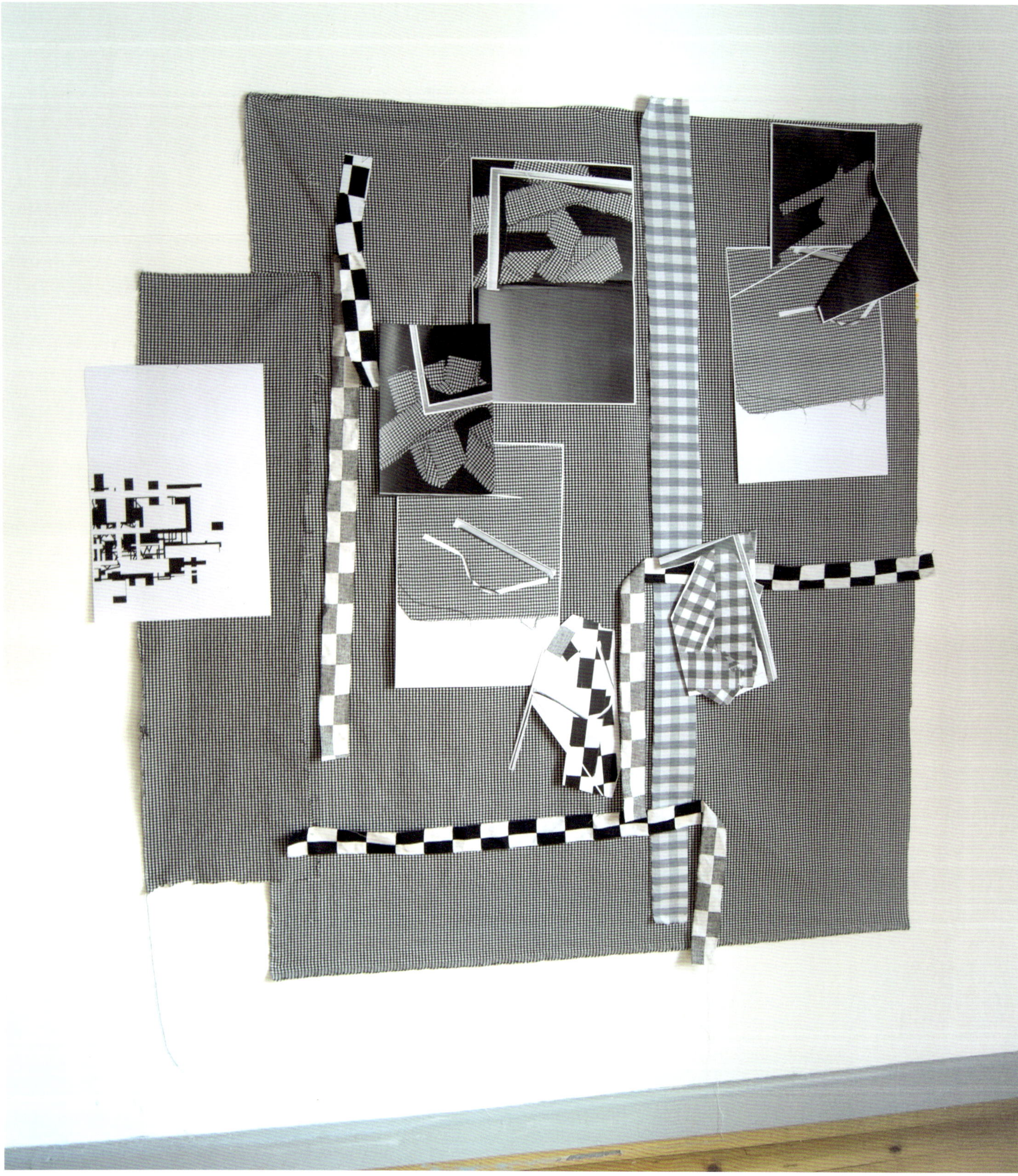

Kar, 2016, checked cloth, photocopies, 150 x 155 cm

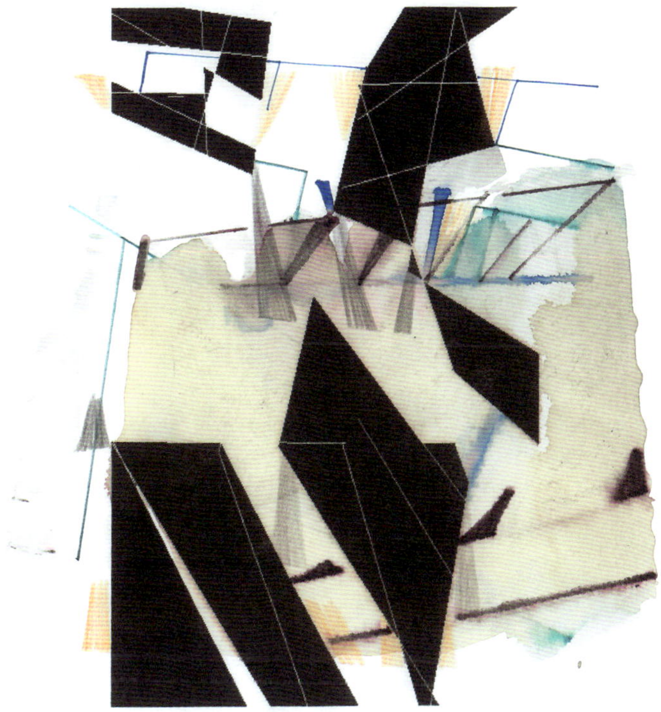

EF2, 2014, water colour, coloured pencil, pencil on digital drawing, 29.7 x 21 cm

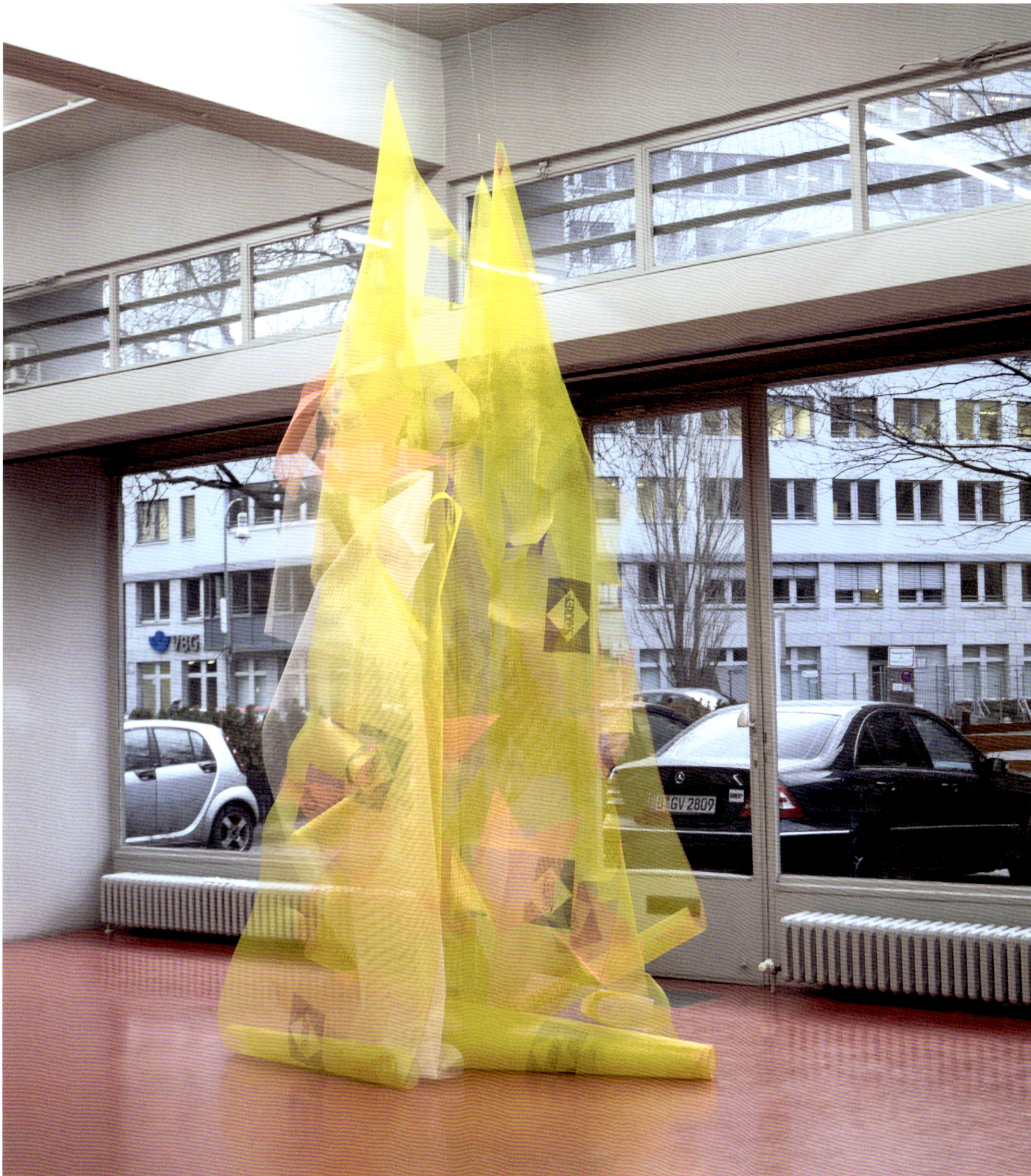

Alaba, 2015, construction nets, dimension variable

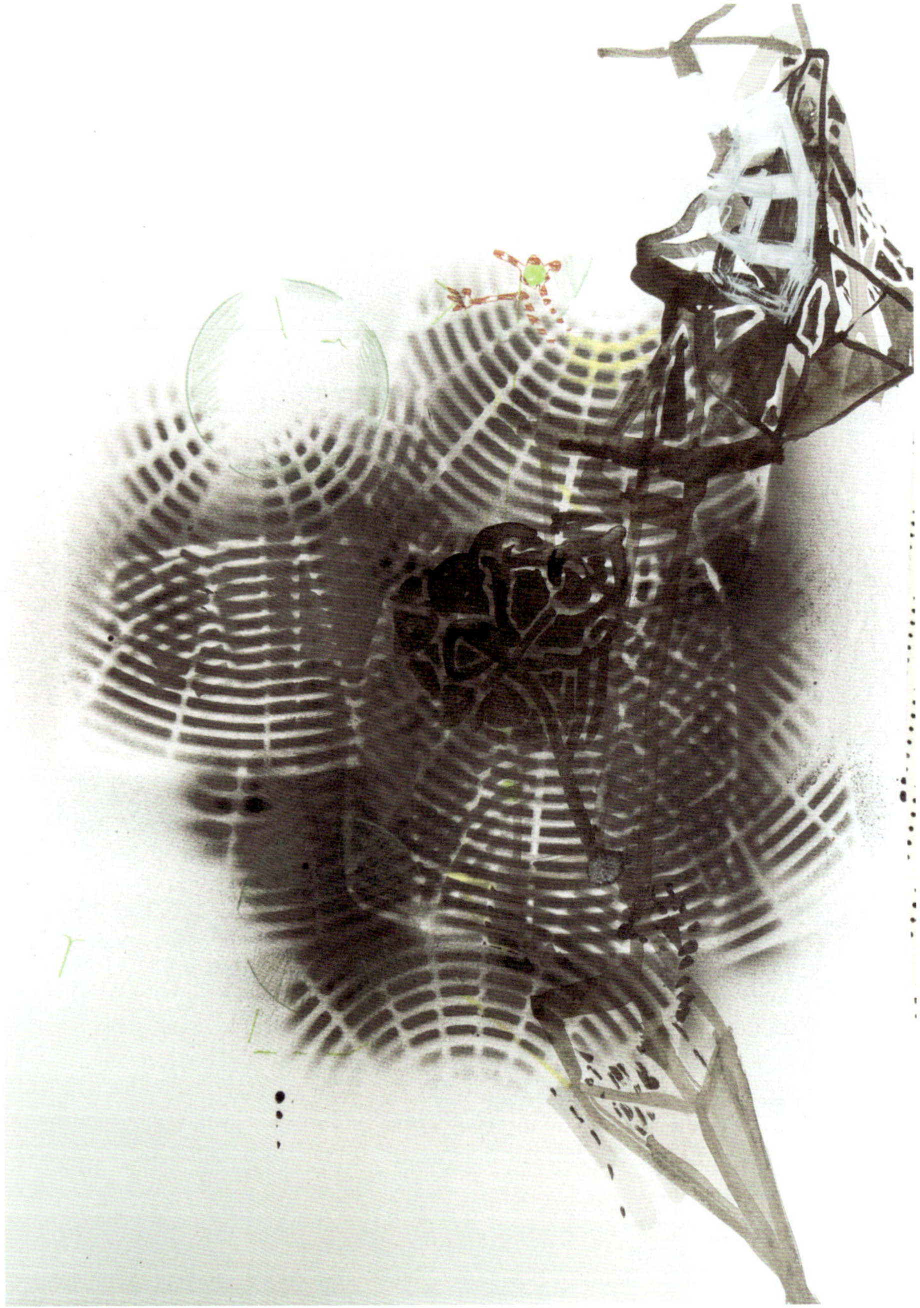

Untitled, 2012, drawing, spray paint, acrylic paint on paper, 55 x 42 cm

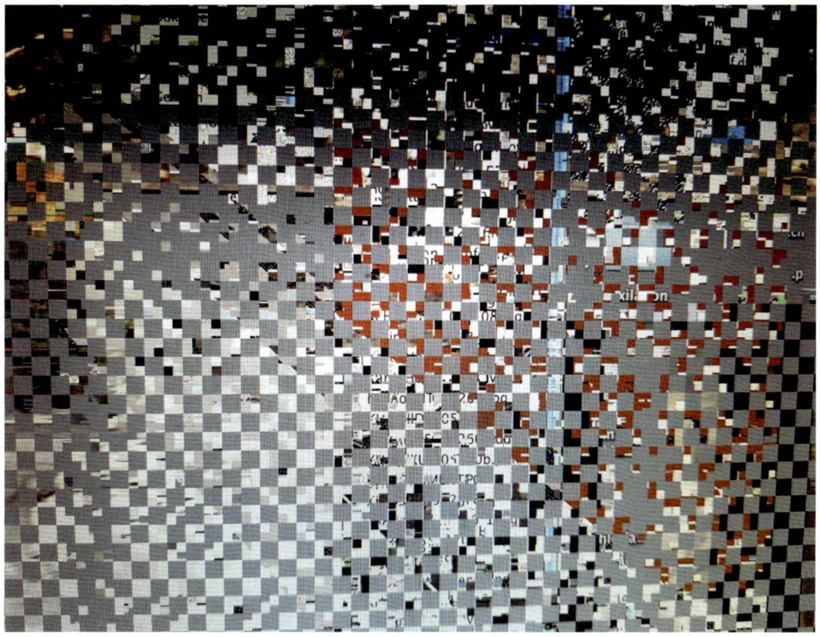

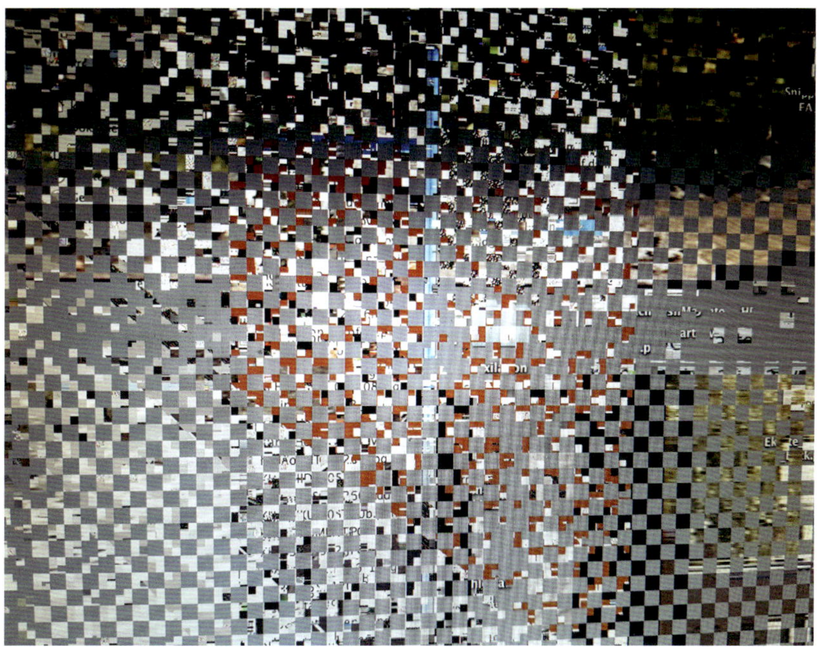

AP 2 (Erxilation), 2018, photography, 30 x 42 cm

AP 1 (Erxilation), 2018, photography, 30 x 42 cm

waw (from the Ggroup), 2018, paper, plaster, polystyrene, graphite, vinylal, 220 x 130 x 100 cm

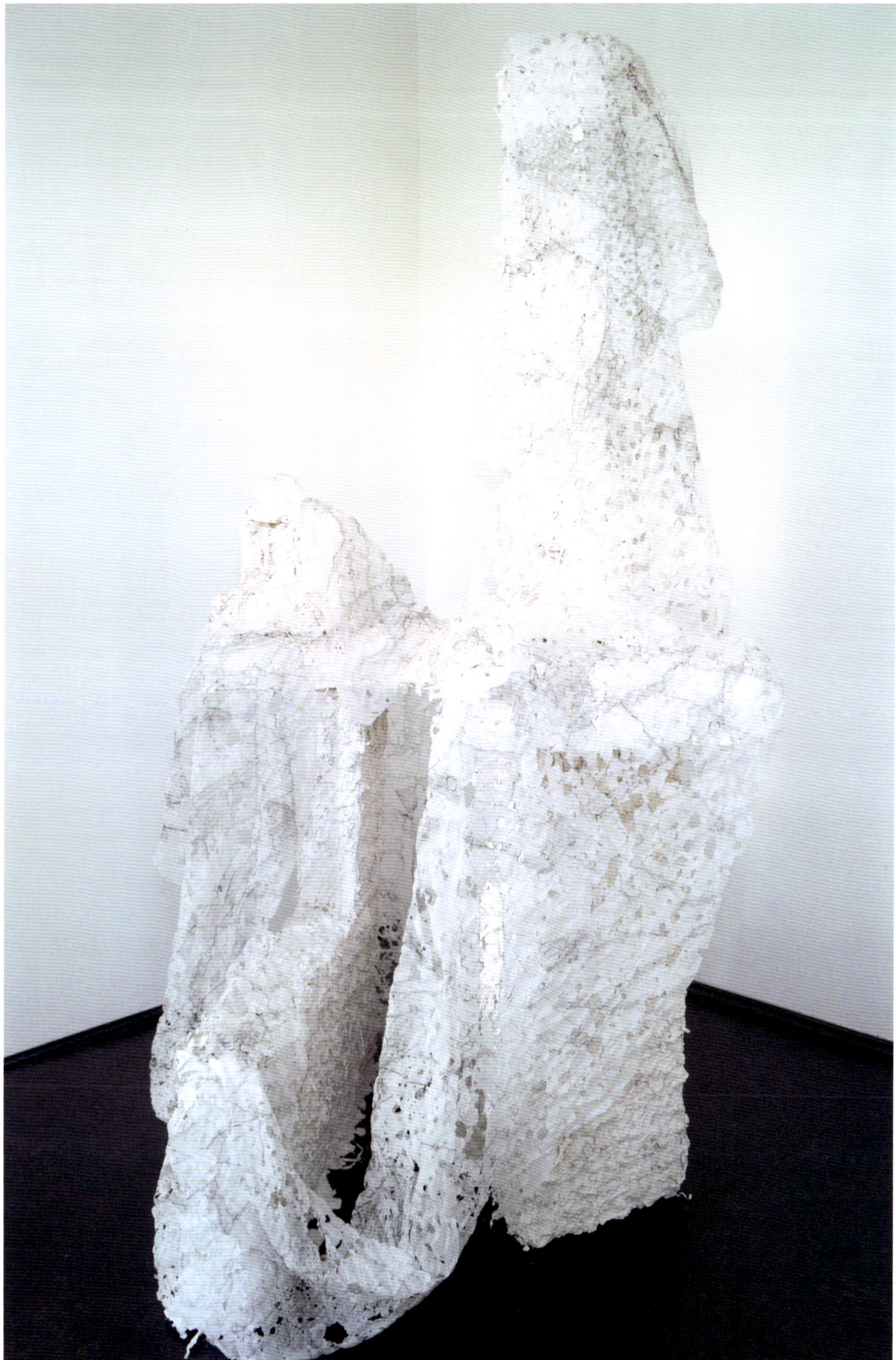

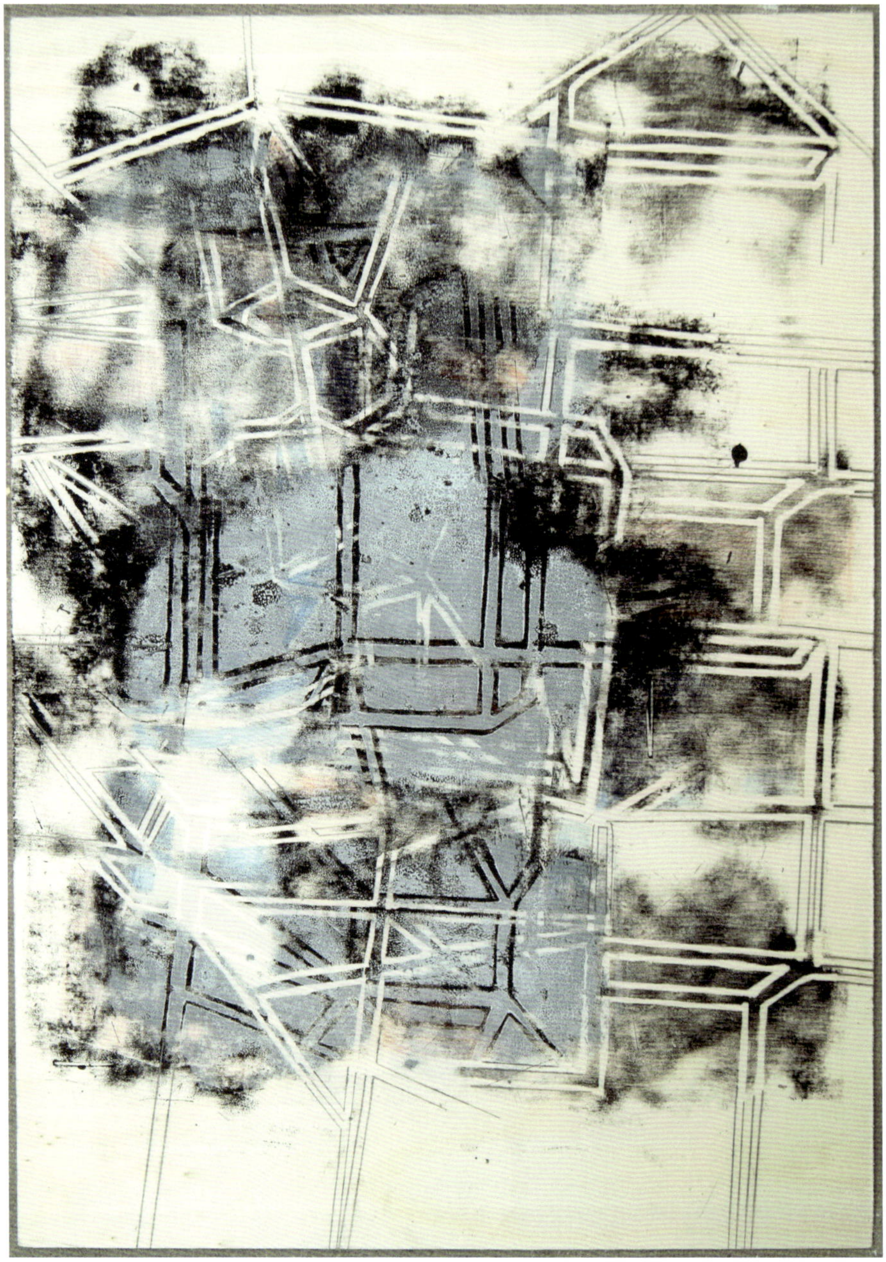

RbrÄ, 2018, linocut and drawing on wood, 40 x 30 cm

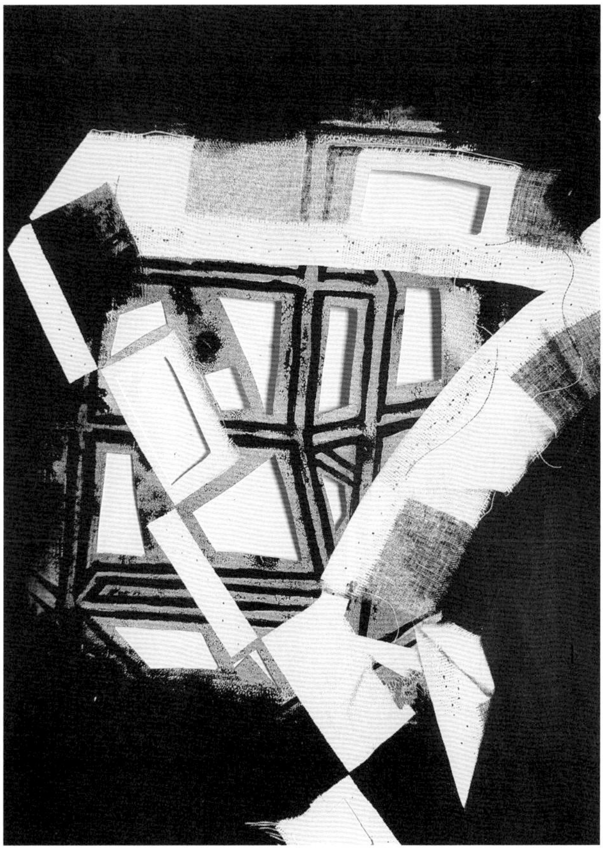

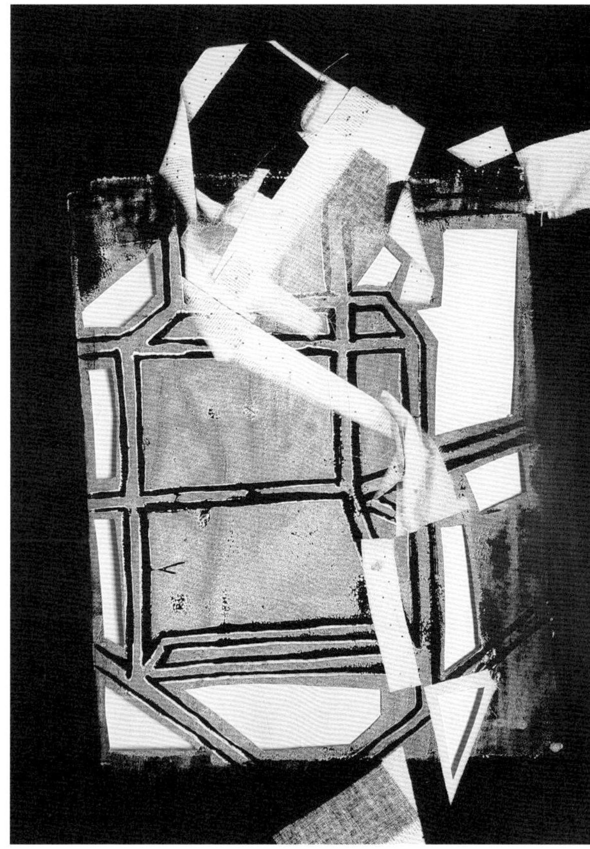

Left: *BE*, 2017, photocopy, linocut, cut-out, 29.7 x 21 cm

Right: *EF*, 2017, photocopy, linocut, cut-out, 29.7 x 21 cm

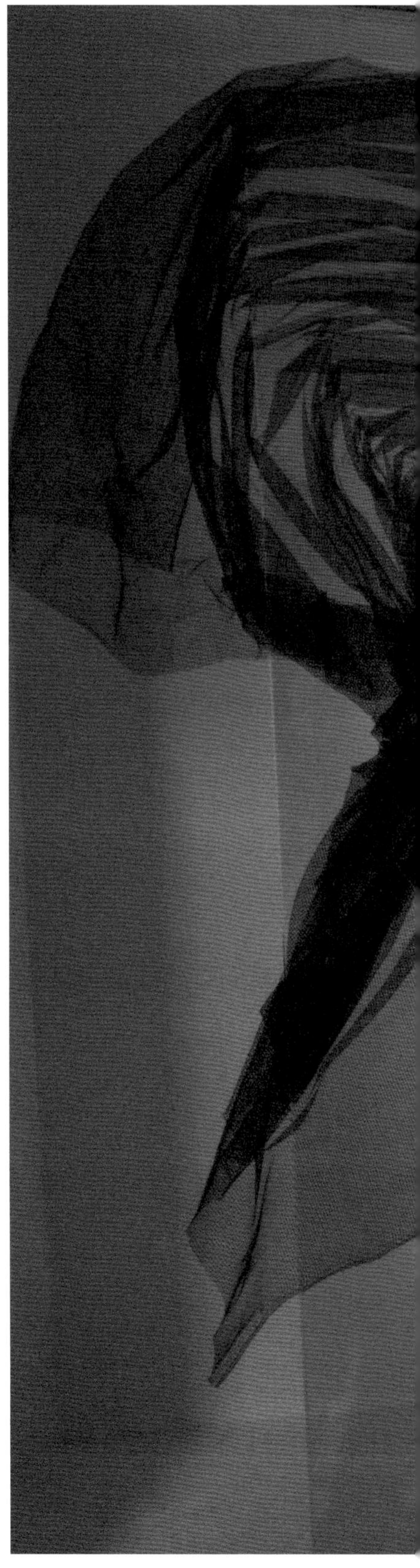

Hub nach Richtung 2, 2019, glass cabinet, fly net, video loop 2 min, colour, without sound, HD 16:9

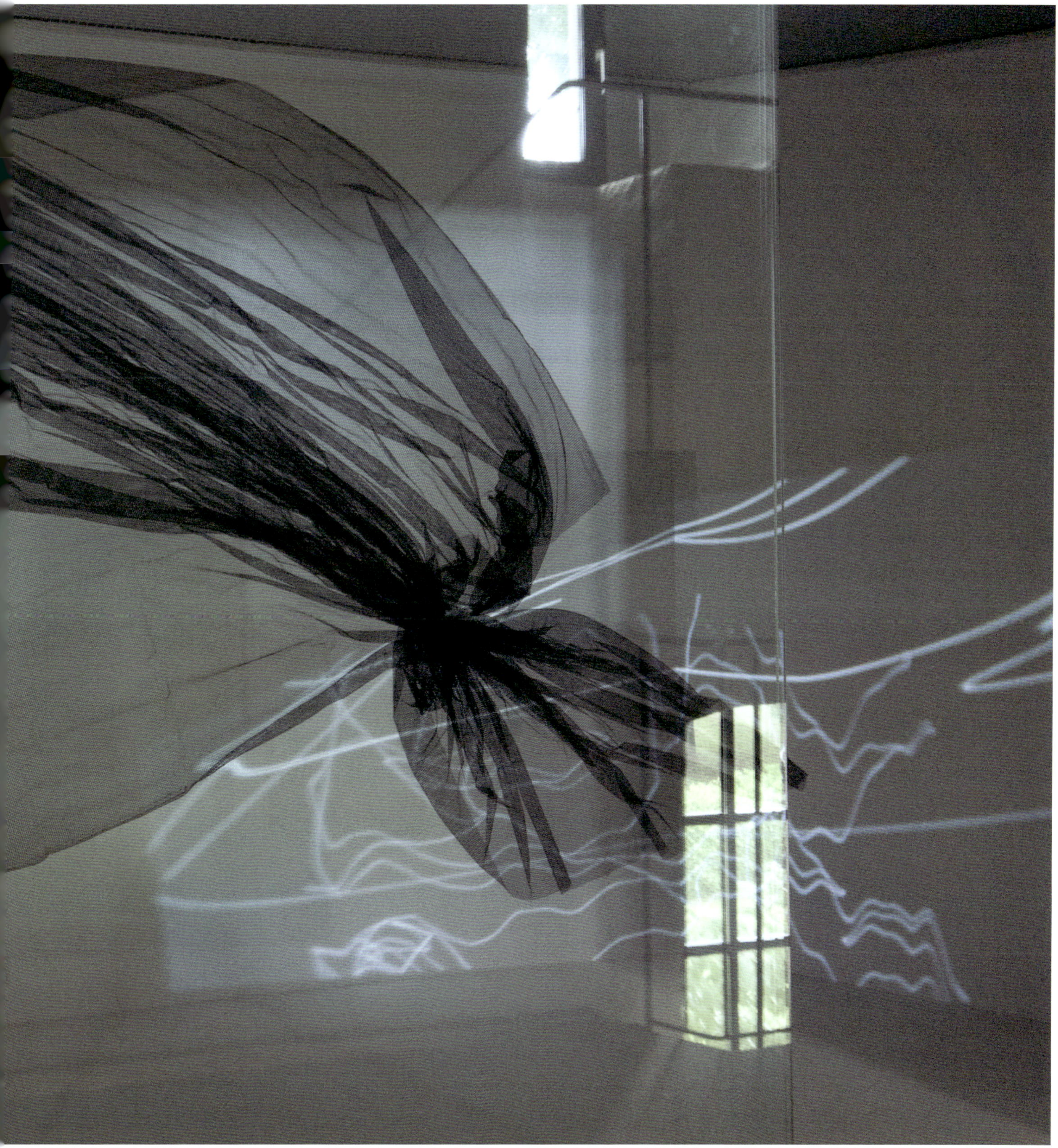

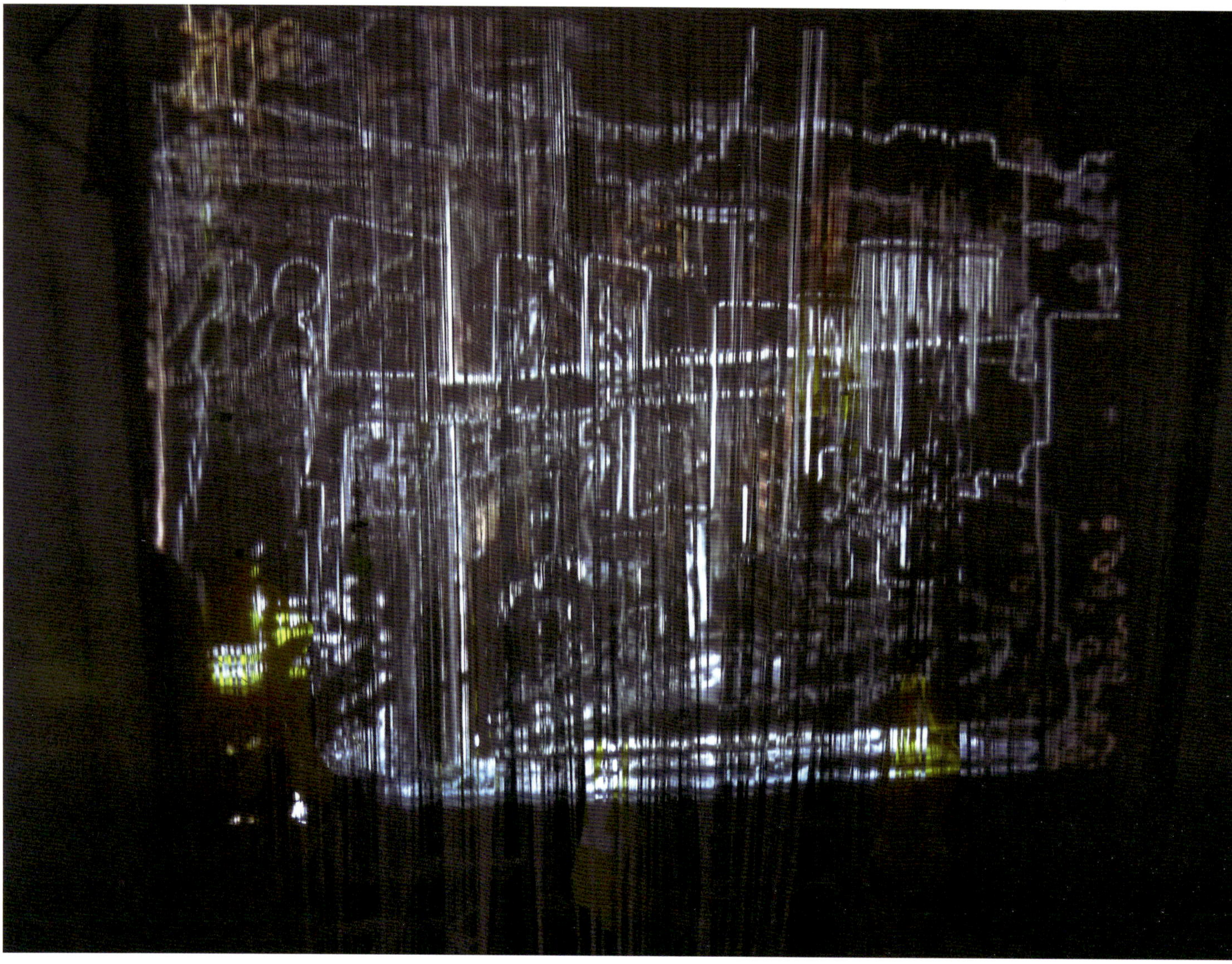

Skop, 2013, installation in a construction wagon, video loop 8:21 min, sound, colour, 4:3, warning vests, thread curtains, fluorescent materials

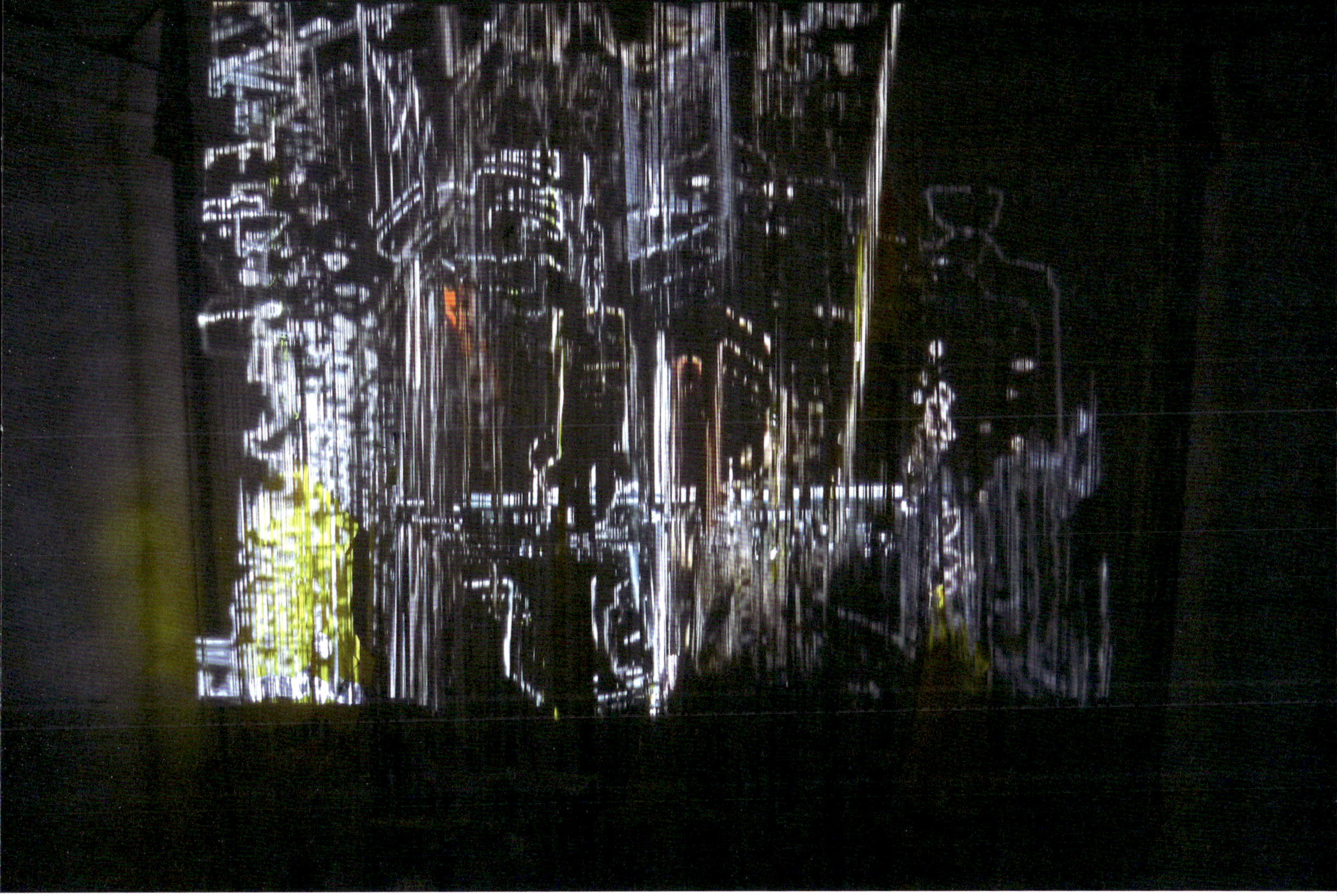

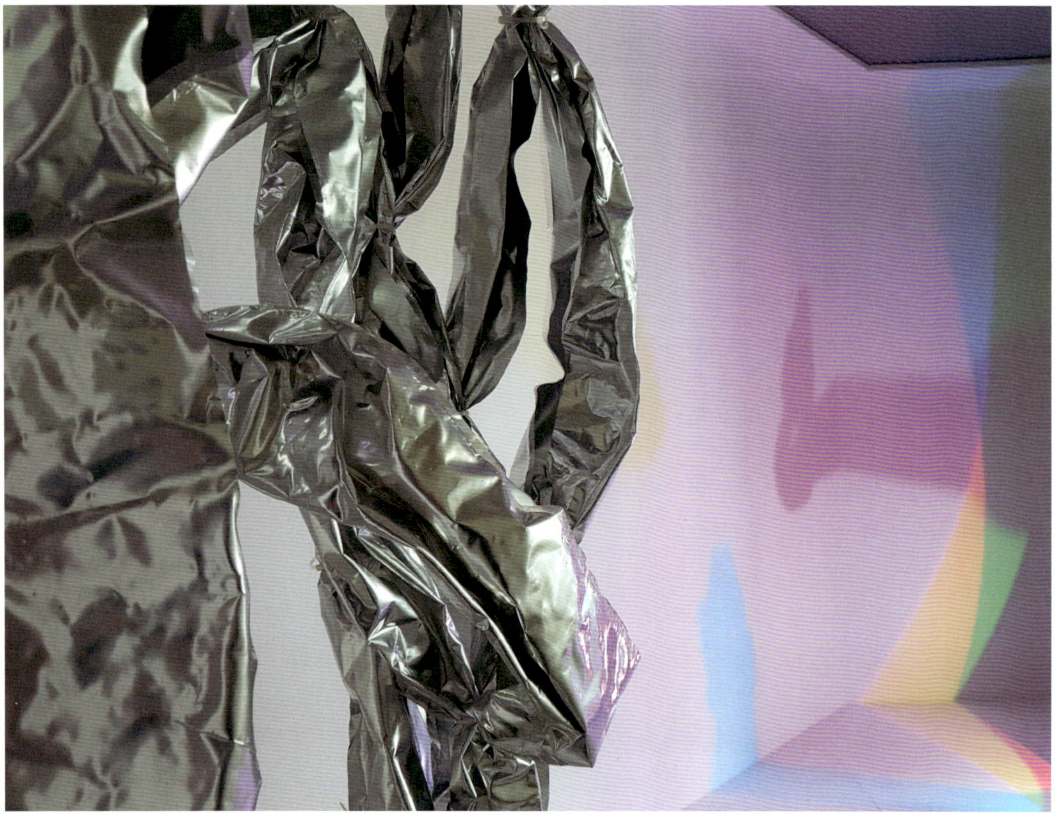

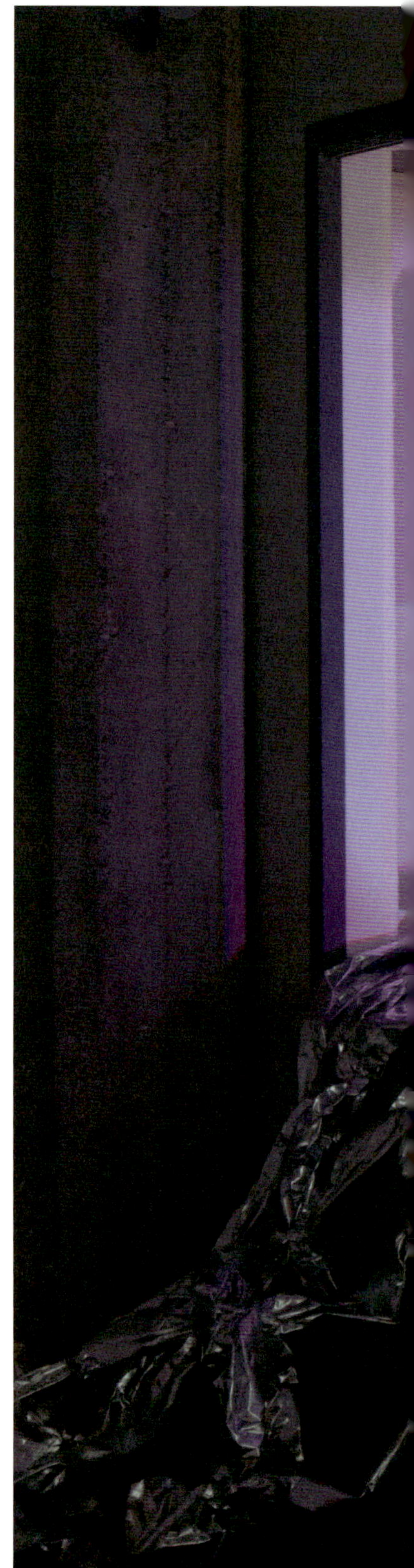

Hub nach Richtung 3, 2019, glass cabinet, foil, prepared colour lamp

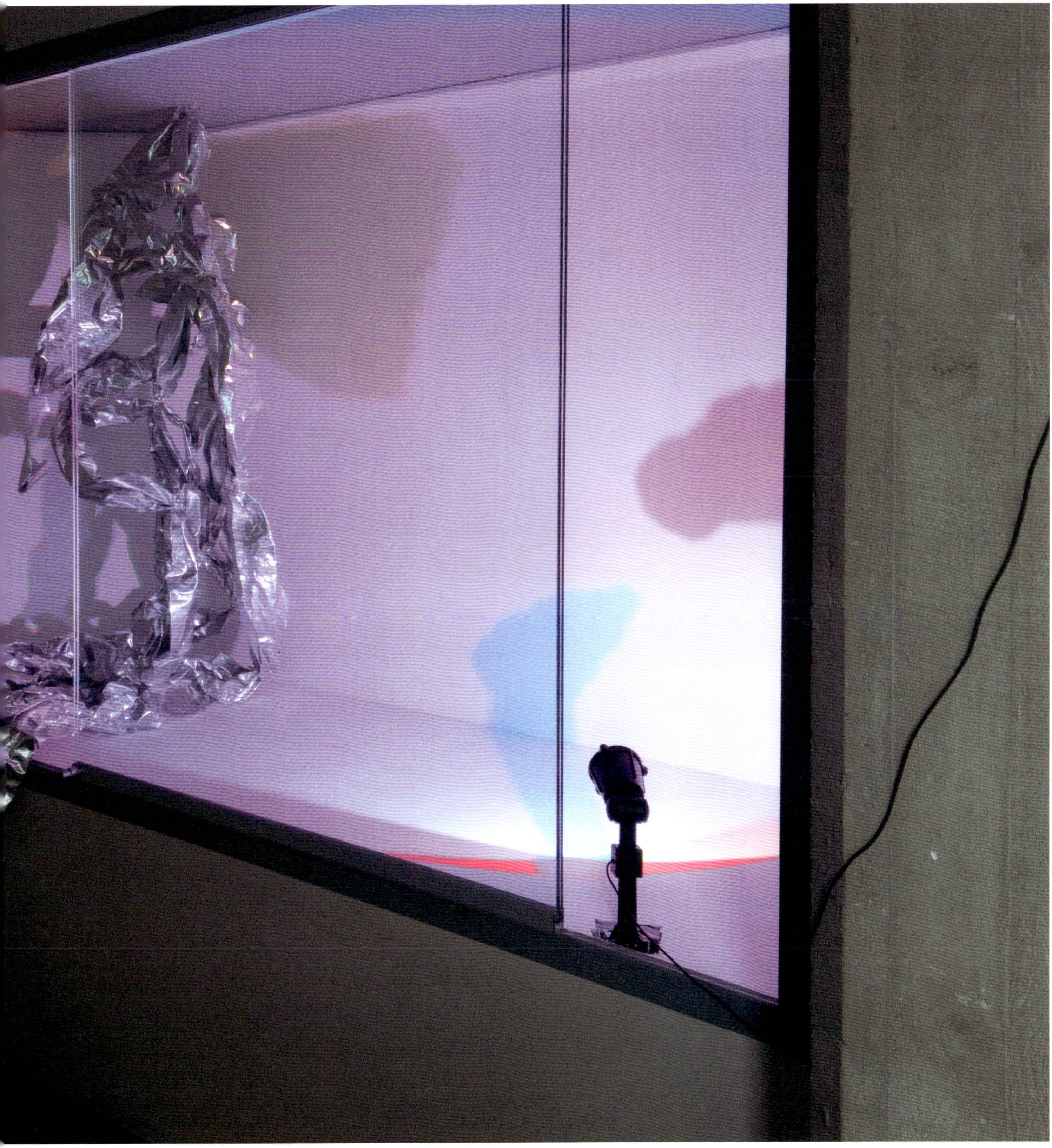

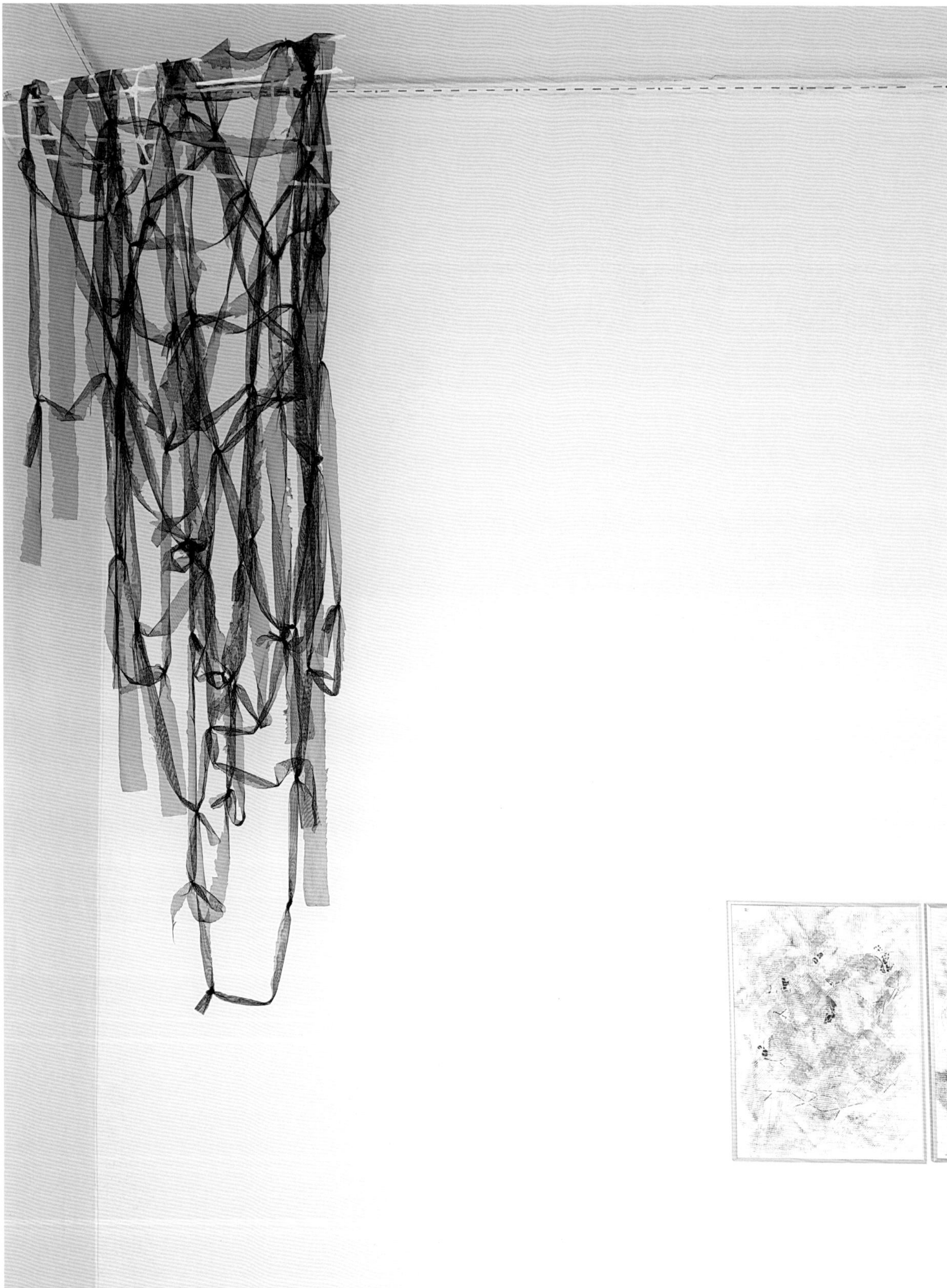

Untitled, 2018, wire, plaster, fly net, dimension variable

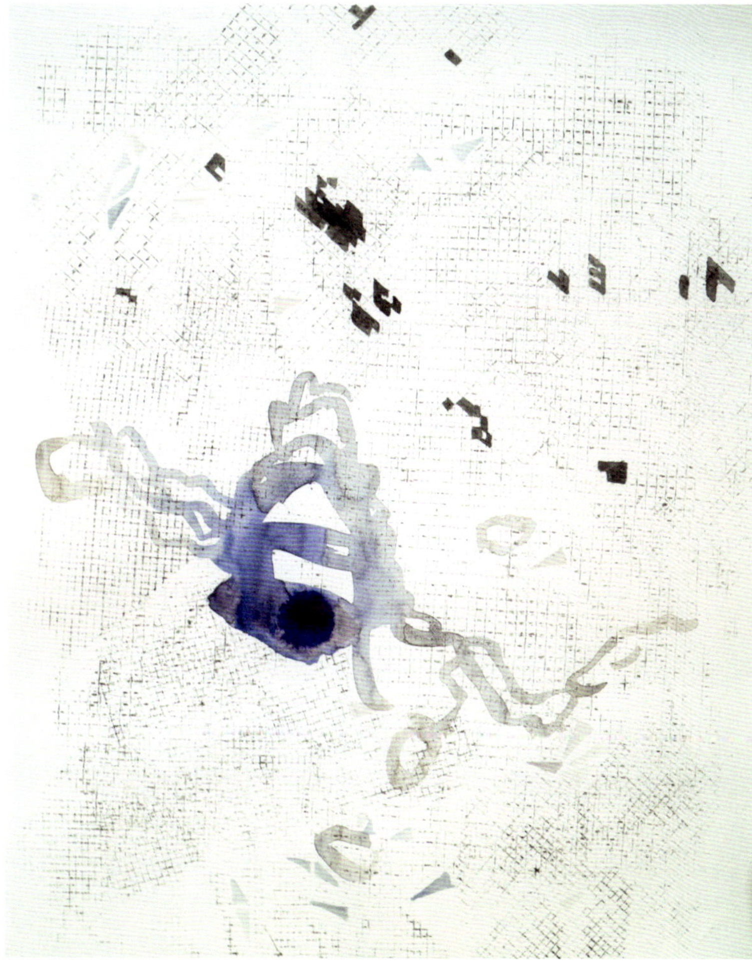

Untitled, 2018, monotype, drawing, watercolour, pigment liner, 65 x 50 cm

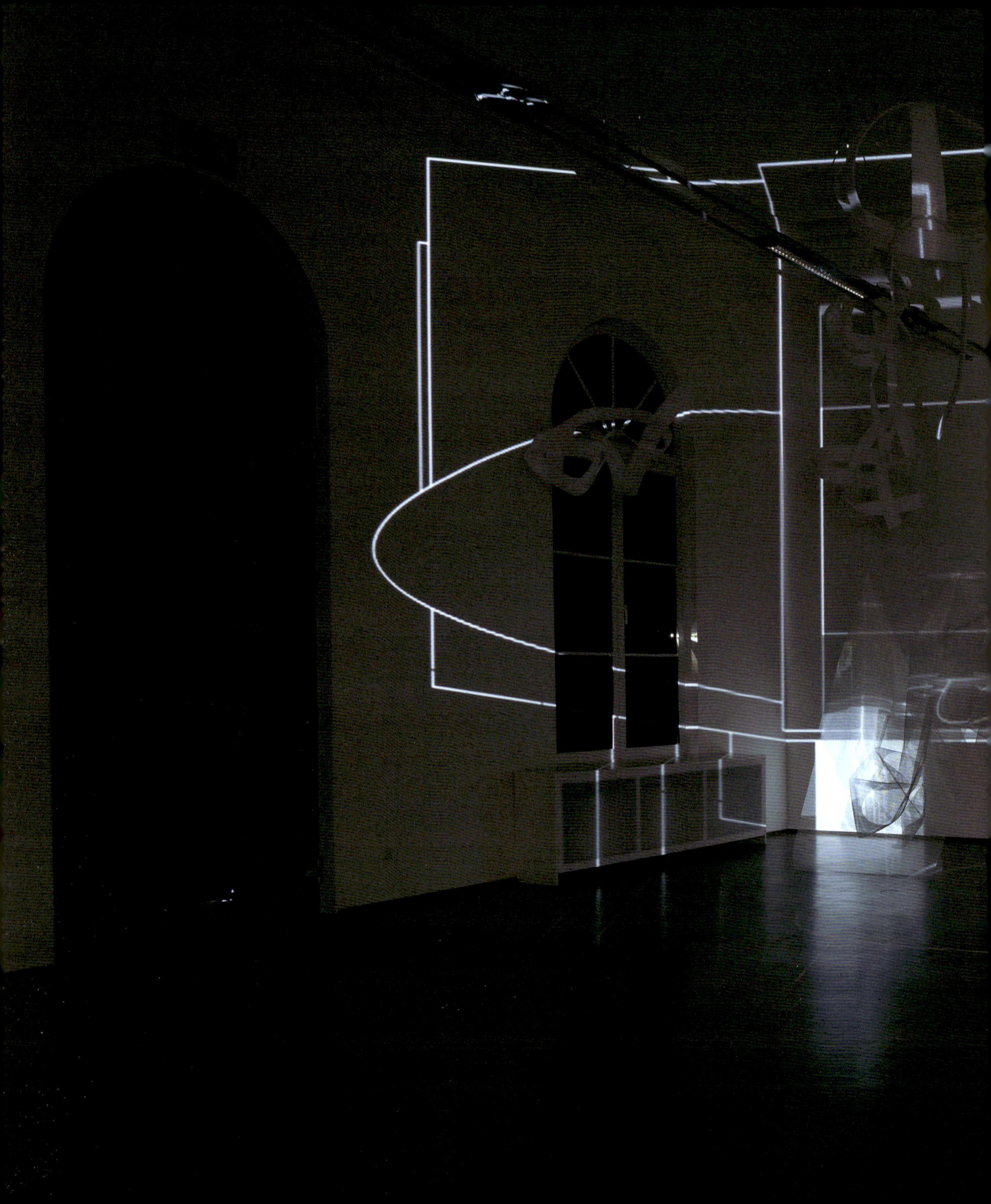

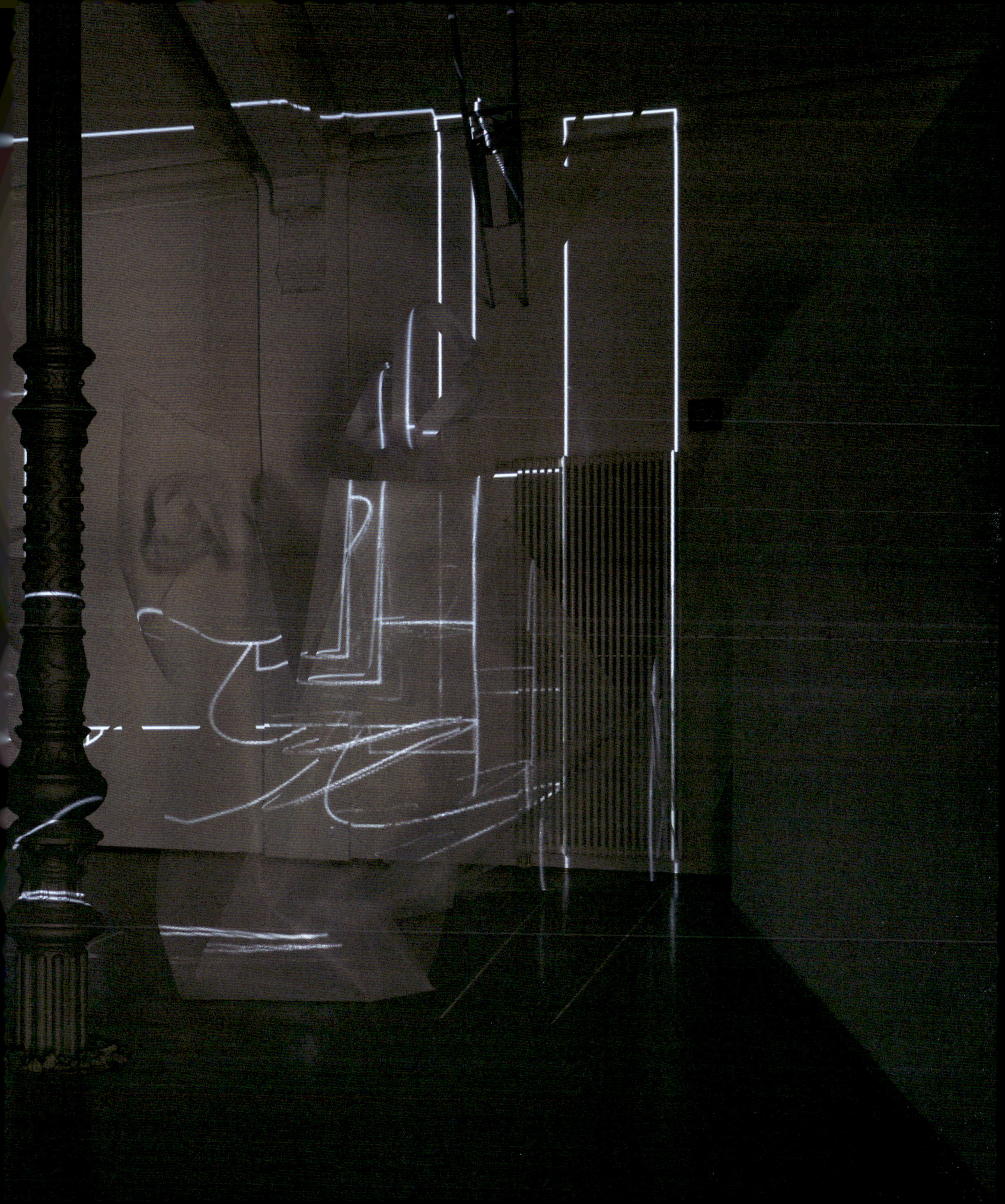

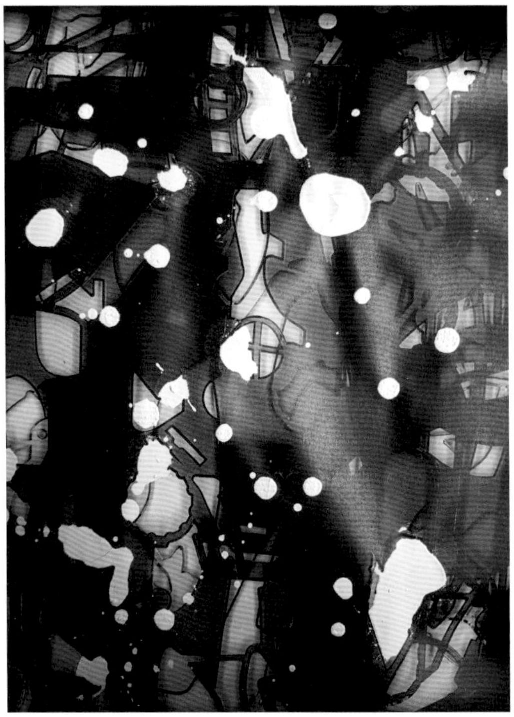

Previous page: *AP*, 2019, photography, 30 x 45 cm

Above and right: *Doppler*, 2019, installation, video loop 2:20 min, colour, sound, HD 16:9, polystyrene, construction nets

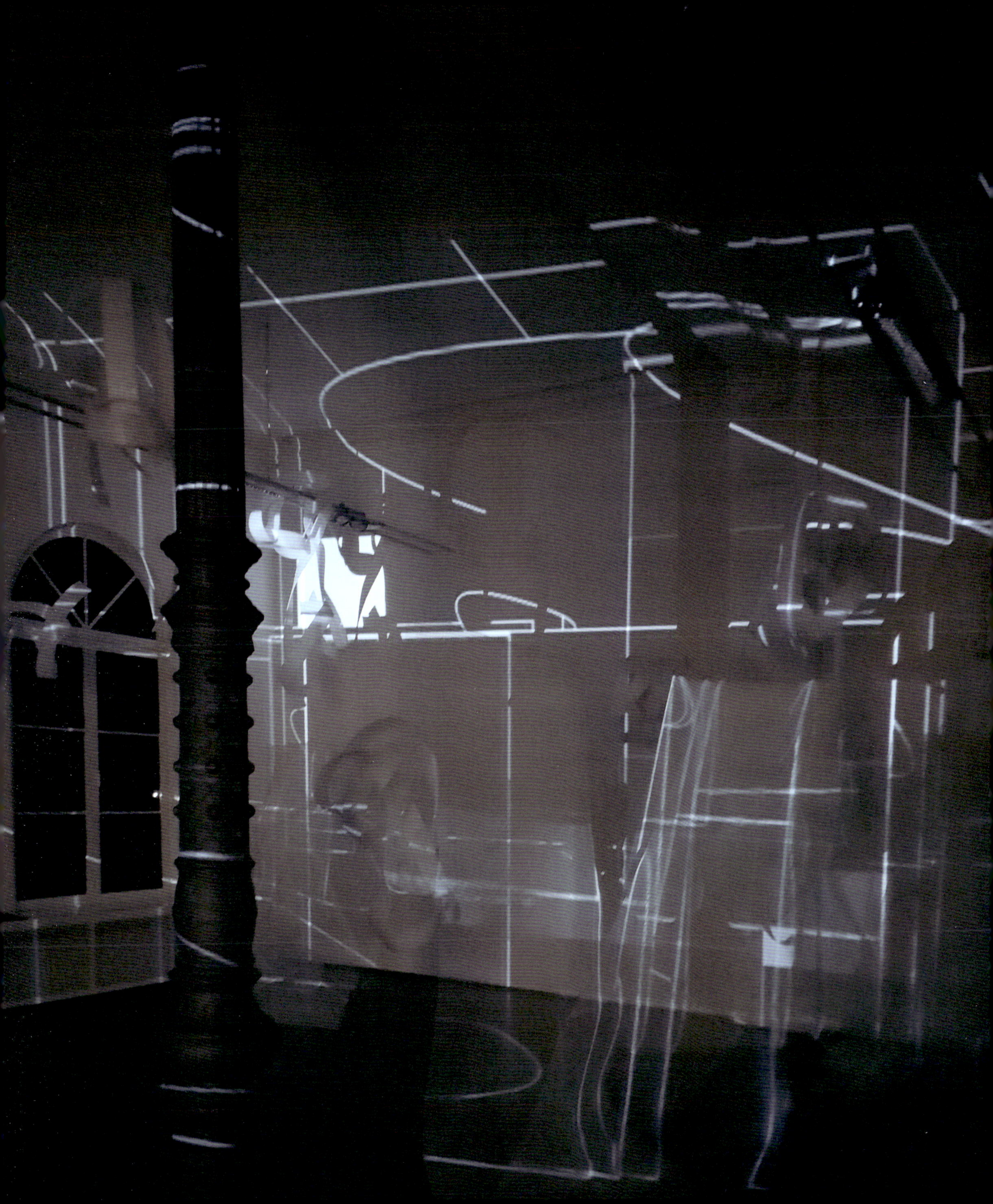

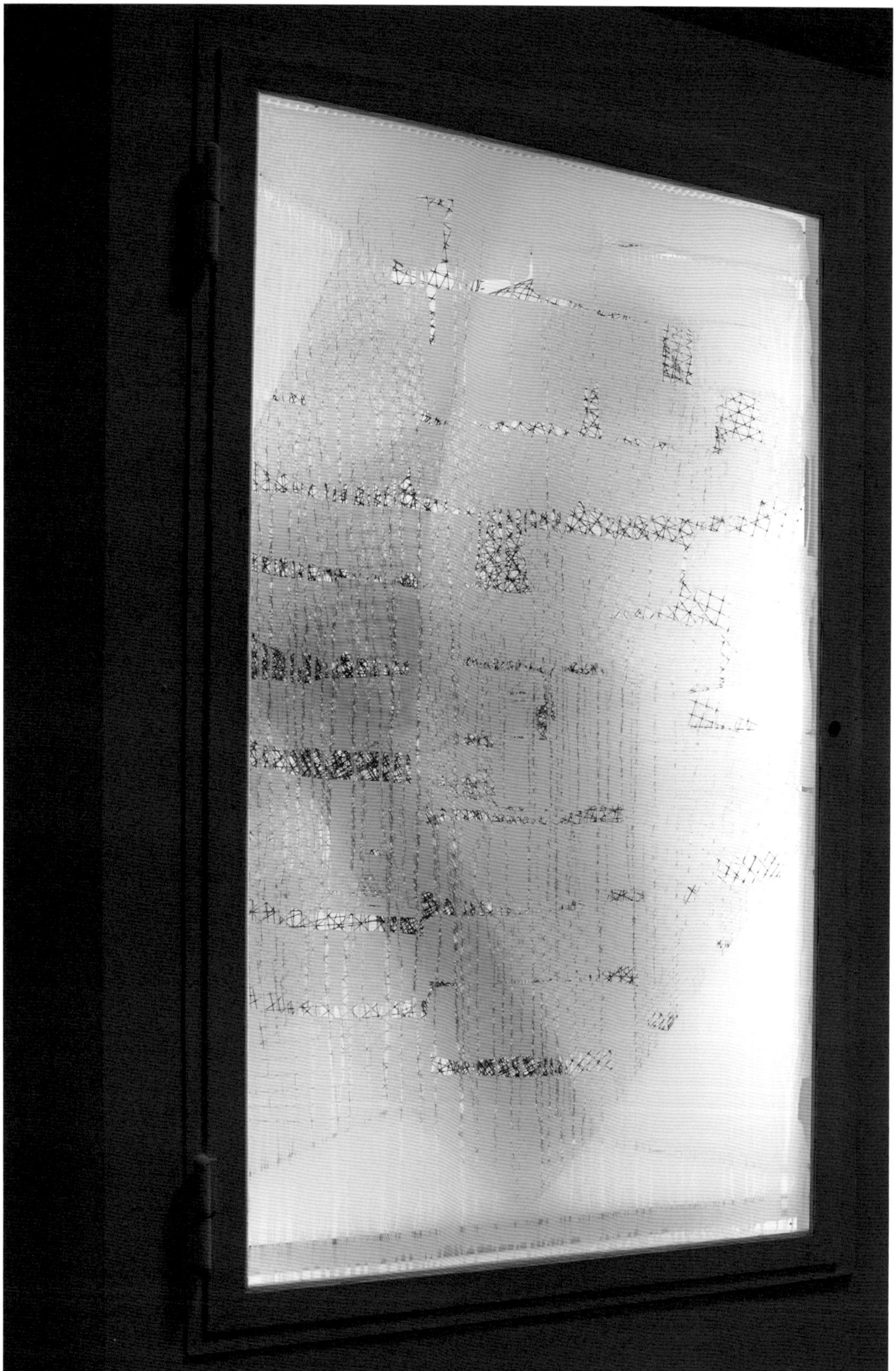

Hub nach Richtung 5, 2019, glass cabinet, net, buttermilk

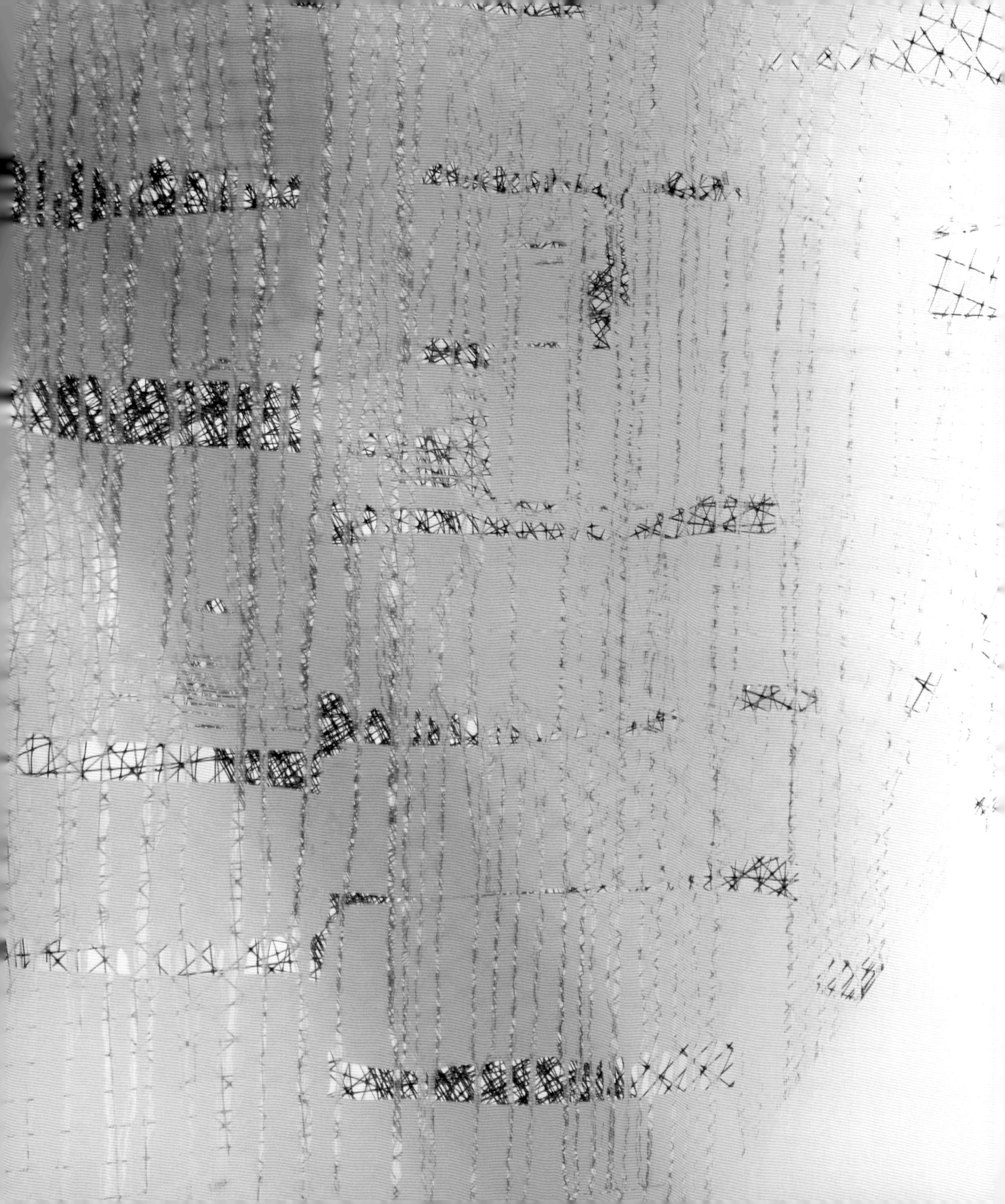

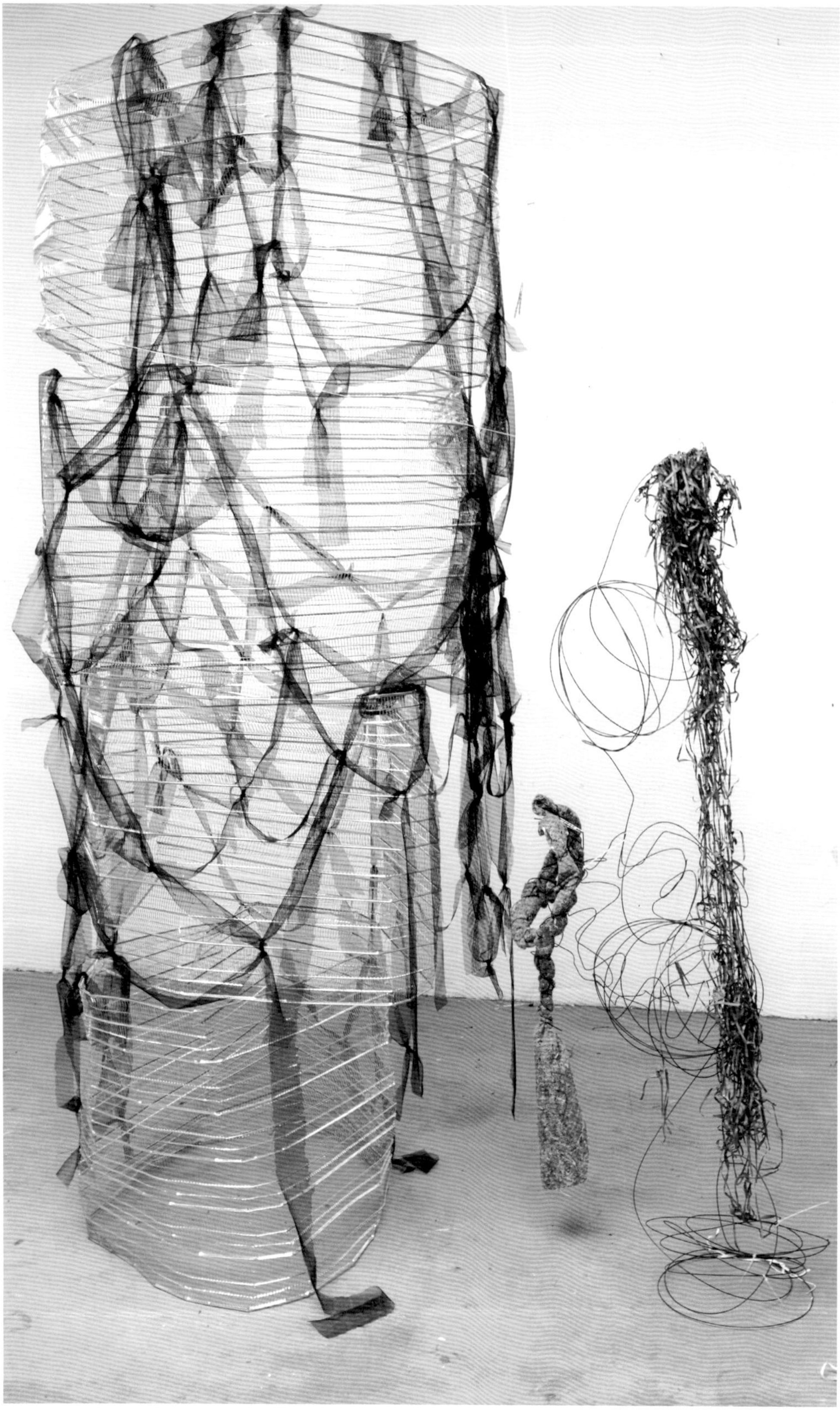

T7b, 2018, metal, net, paper, cloth, wire, 220 x 100 x 80 cm

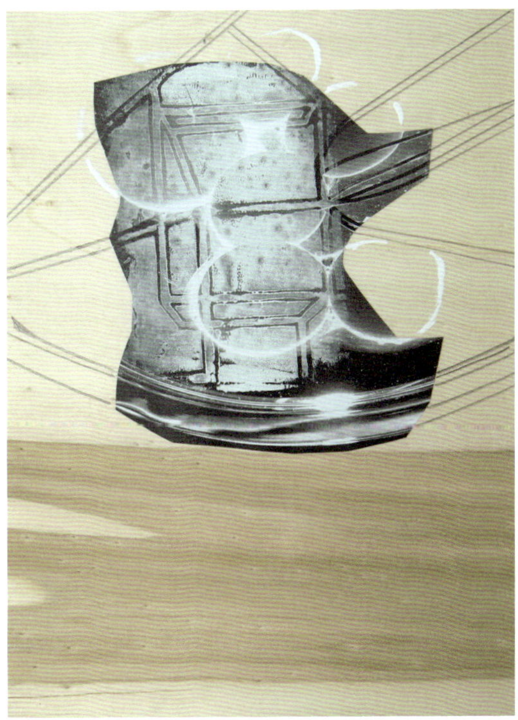

RBrÄ12, 2018, pencil, linocut, photocopy on wood, 40 x 30 cm

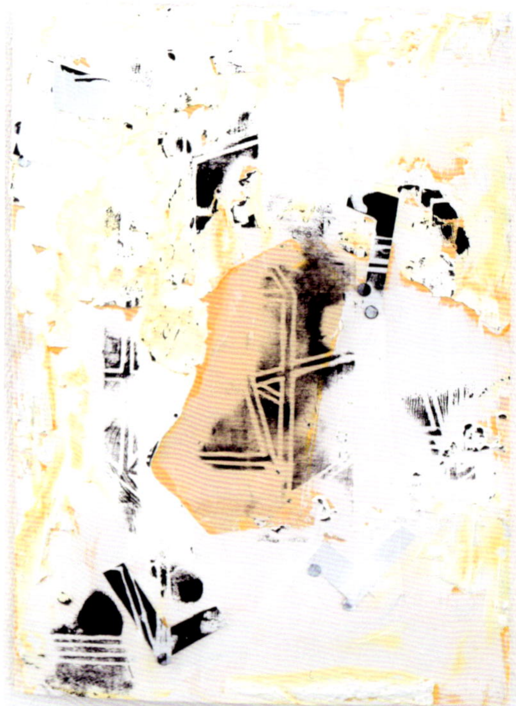

Above: *RBrÄ5*, 2018, ink, plaster, linocut on wood, 40 x 30 cm

Right: *Untitled*, 2019, watercolour, ink, pencil, pigment liner on paper, 100 x 70 cm

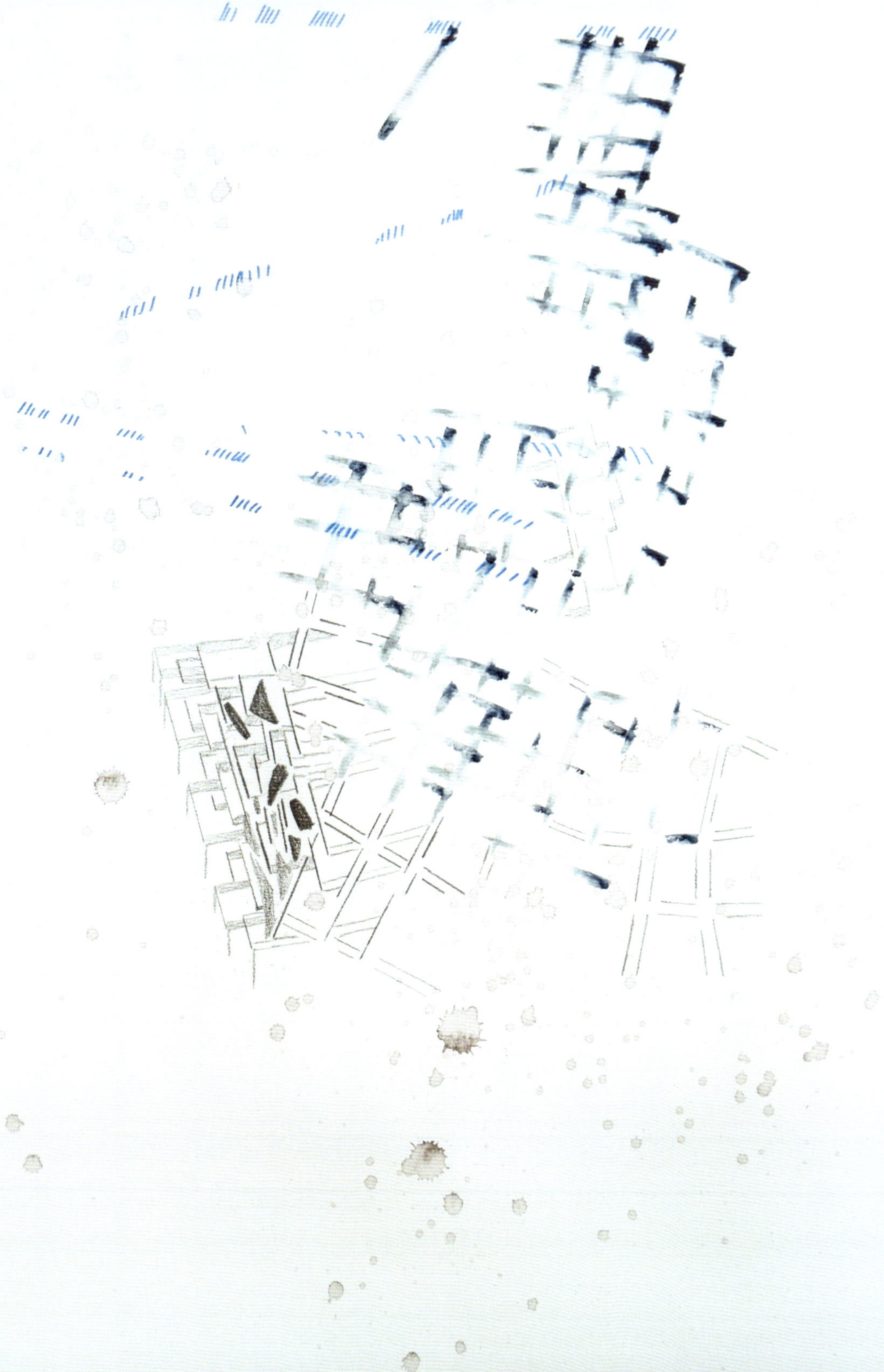

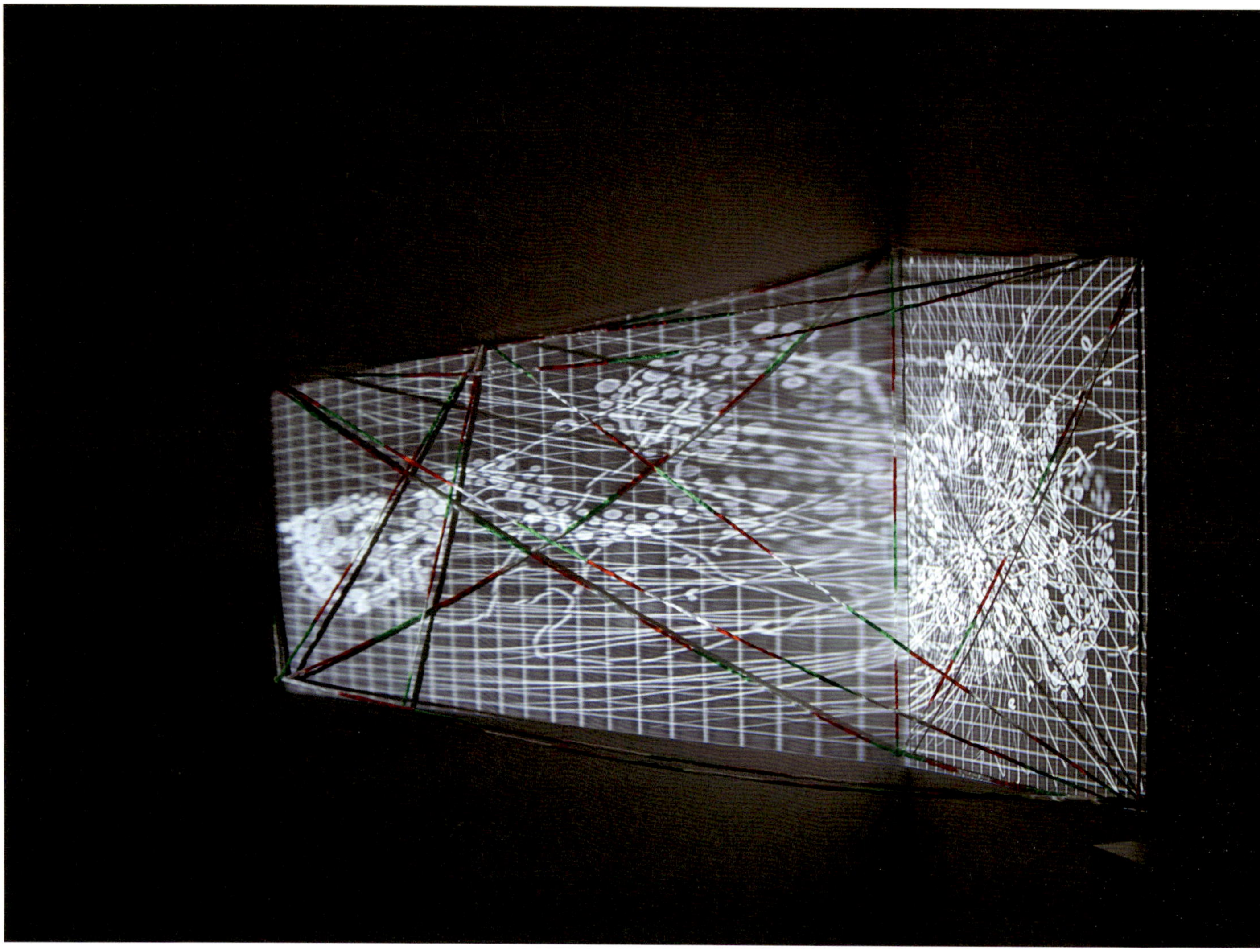

Zeia, 2019, video loop 1:42 min, colour, without sound, HD 16:9, yarn

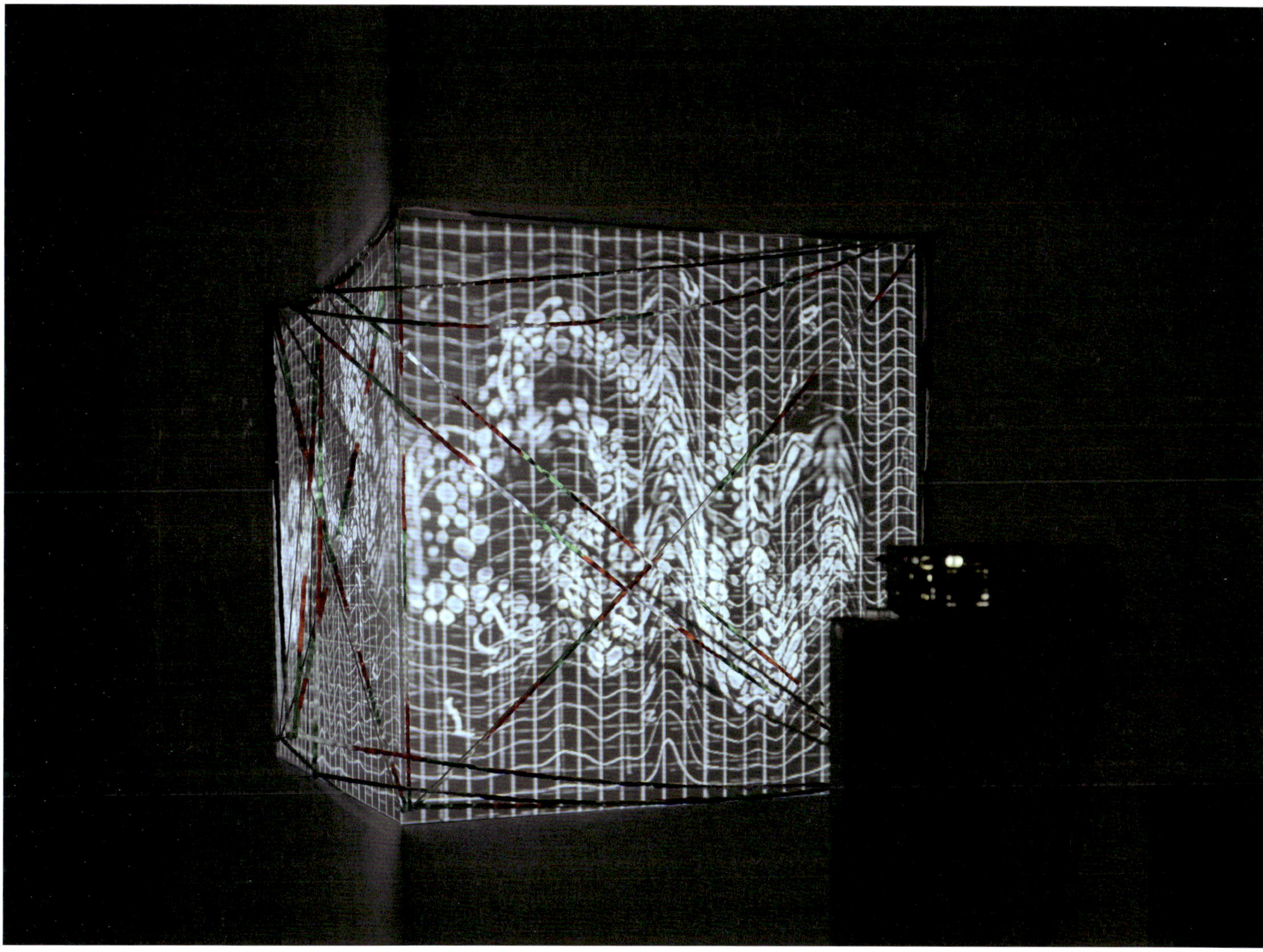

Svie, 2017, overhead projector, cut-out drawing, net, dimension variable

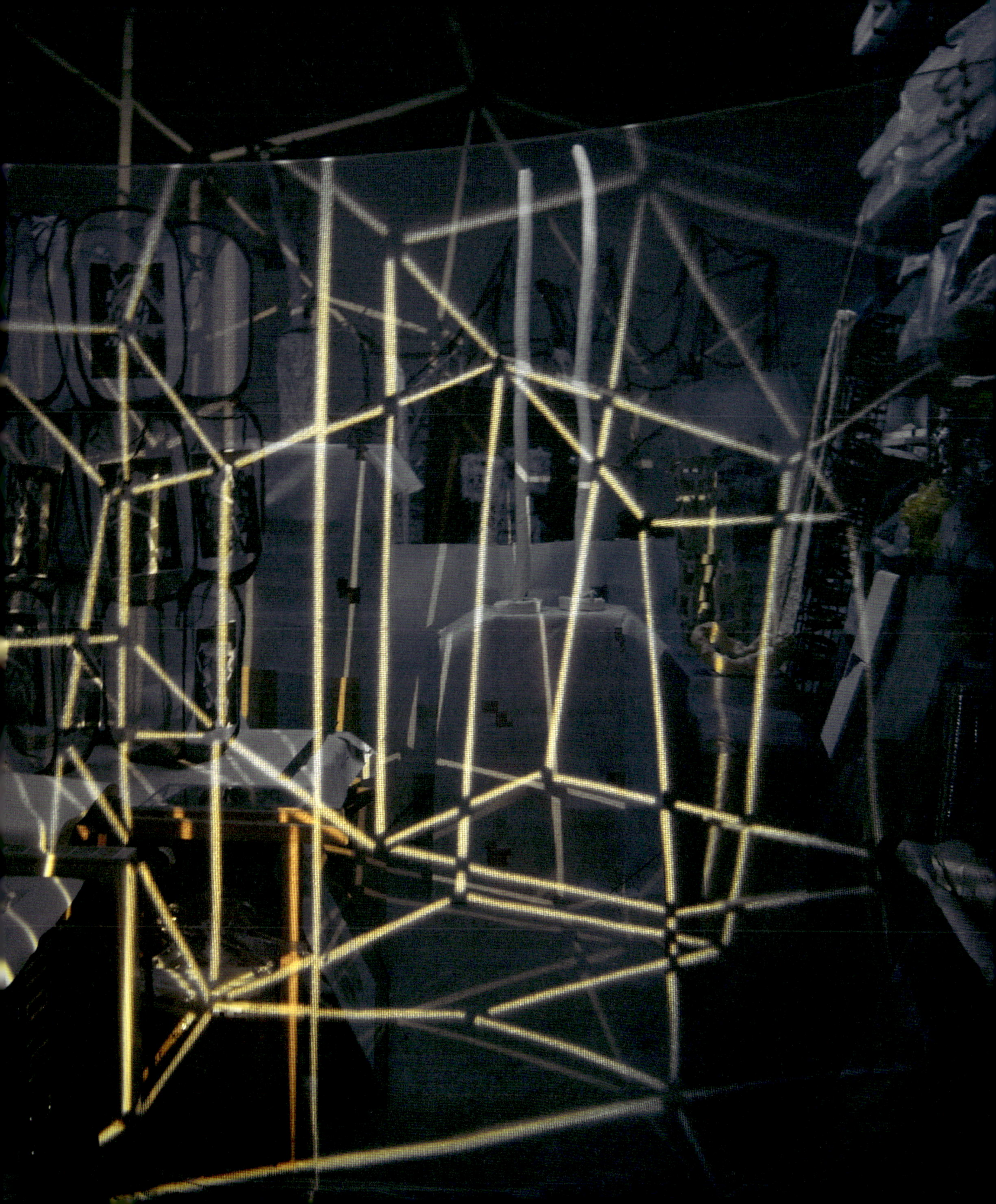

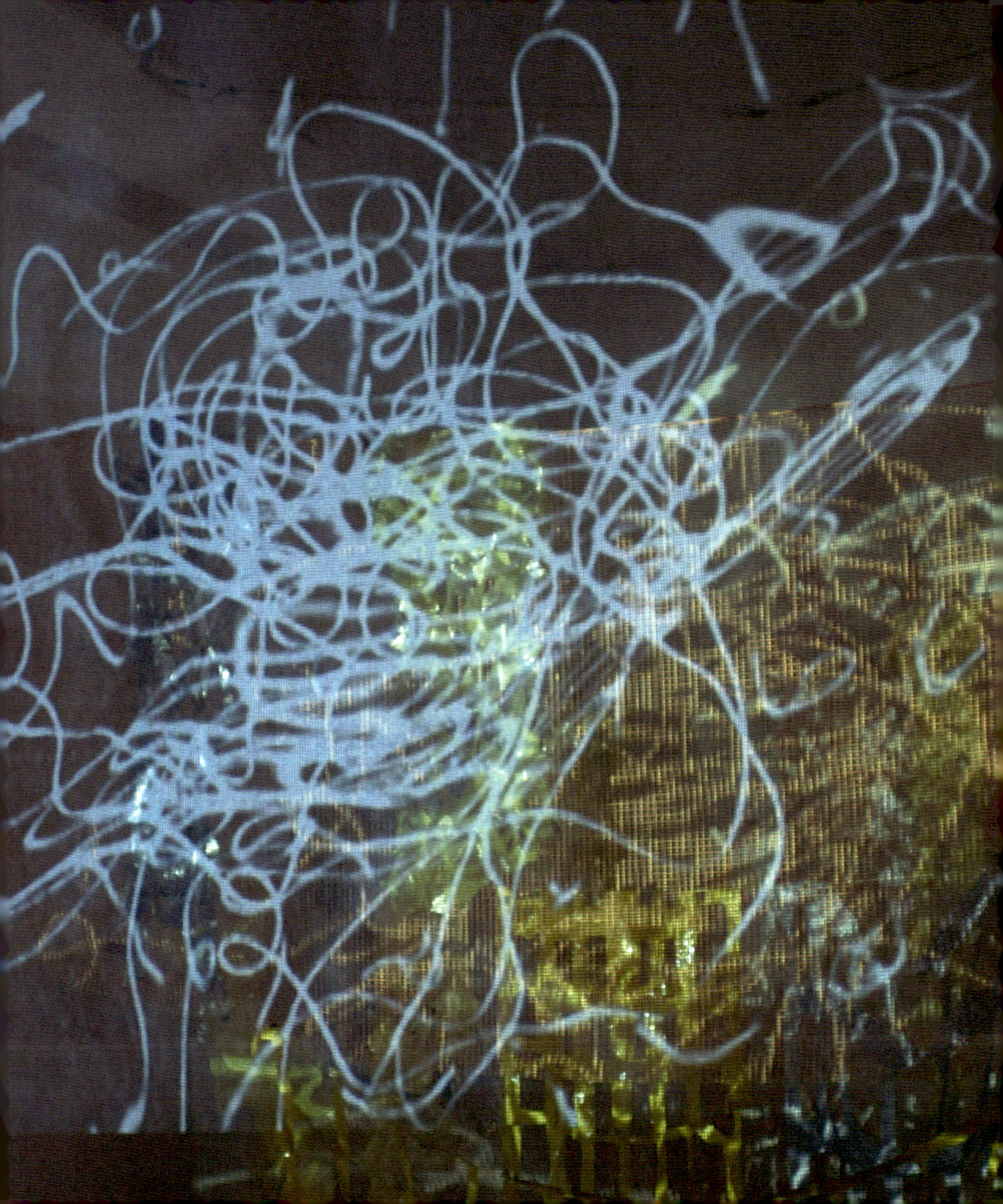

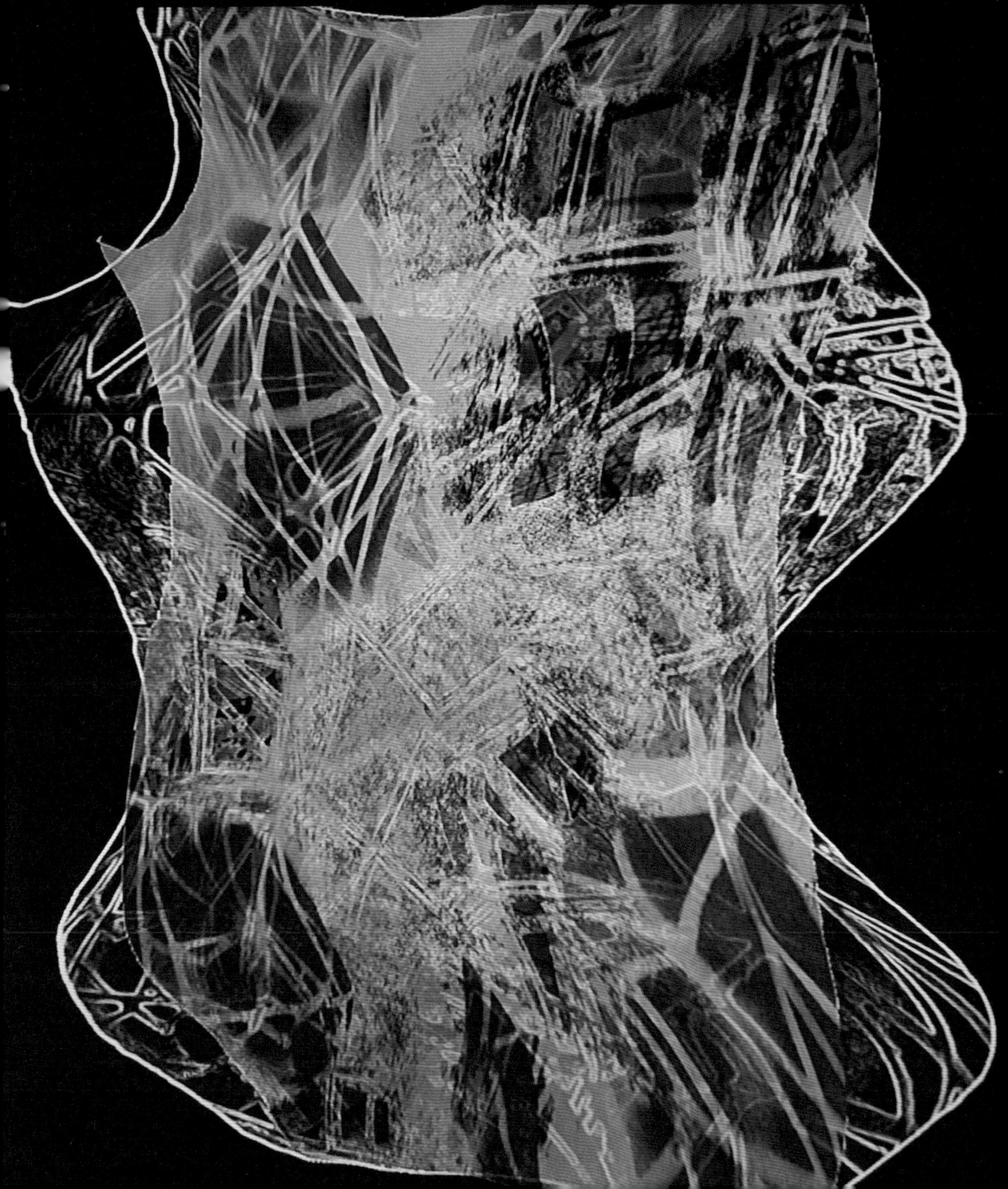

Biography

1960
Born in Cologne (D)
1980–85
Studies Fine Arts at the Staatliche Kunstakademie Düsseldorf (D) (Sculpture, Photography, Video/Film, Drawing, Mixed Media)
1985
Meisterschülerin (Diploma) Fine Arts of Prof Franz Eggenschwiler
1980–87
Studies Pedagogy of Fine Arts and Philosophy at Staatliche Kunstakademie Düsseldorf and Heinrich-Heine-Universität Düsseldorf (D)
1991–94
Studies Ancient History and Archaeology at Universität zu Köln, Cologne (D)

Grants, Awards

2019
Publication Support by Stiftung Kunstfonds, Bonn (D)
2016
Residency at the Stiftung Bartels Fondation, Basel (CH)
2007
Working scholarship at the European Ceramic Work Centre, Den Bosch (NL)
2000
Working scholarship in London (UK), awarded by the Ministry of Culture and Science of the State of North Rhine-Westphalia (D)
1997
Laureate of the Augenblicke Prize awarded by the Optica, Cologne (D)
1996
Project grant of the Colegio Oficial de Arquitectos de Málaga (E), invited to Mediterranean Symposium by AIAP and UNESCO, Paris (F)
Friedrich-Vordemberge Prize awarded by the City of Cologne (D)
1992
Working scholarship in Olevano Romano (I), Villa Massimo, awarded by the Ministry of Culture and Science of the State of North Rhine-Westphalia (D)
1990
Ringenberg Grant awarded by the State of North Rhine-Westphalia (D)
1989
Peter-Mertes Grant awarded by the Bonner Kunstverein (D)
1988
Project scholarship in Civitella d'Agliano (I), awarded by Kunstfonds e. V., Bonn (D)

Teaching, Lectures, Artist Talks

since 2019
Lectureship (Photography, Contemporary Illustration) at Rheinische Fachhochschule Köln, Cologne (D)
2017
Lectureship (Drawing) at Hochschule Mainz (D)
2010–17
Lectureship at the ZEW of Leibniz University Hannover (D)
2016
The Dialogue#11, Artist Talk at Stiftung Bartels Fondation, Basel (CH)
2015
Artist talk at the onomato künstlerverein e. V., Düsseldorf (D)
2014
Artist talk and lecture at Siena Art Institute Onlus (I)
Adjunct/Associate Professor (Visual Thinking) for the Loyola Marymount University, Los Angeles (US) at AIB, Akademie für Internationale Bildung, Bonn (D)
2006/07
Visiting Professorship (Drawing and Installation) at the HBK, Hochschule für Bildende Künste Braunschweig (D)
2006/05/02/01
Lectureship at the Academy of Fine Arts of the Johannes Gutenberg-Universität Mainz (D)
2002–04
Visiting Professorship at the Academy of Fine Arts of the Johannes Gutenberg-Universität Mainz (D)
1998
Lectureship (Sculpture) at the Goethe-Universität Frankfurt am Main (D)

Selected Solo Exhibitions

2020
gegengerade, Galerie Ulrich Mueller, Cologne (D)
2019
Kepler - 452b (with Nicola Schrudde), Forum für Kunst und Kultur Herzogenrath e. V. (D)
Hub nach Richtung (with Katja Butt), Museum Zündorfer Wehrturm, Cologne (D)
2018
per se, Galerie Ulrich Mueller, Cologne (D)
2016
Et prend aux serieux les fantômes, Museumsnacht, Kulturbunker Köln, Cologne (D)
ringsum, Stiftung Bartels Fondation, Basel (CH)
Phi, Moltkerei Werkstatt e. V., Cologne (D)
2015
continuum, Kunstverein Mönchengladbach e. V. (D) (Cat.)
2013
Skop, KWmobil, Kunstmuseen Krefeld (D)
2012
Desolate Sculpture, KunstWerk e. V., Cologne (D)

2008/09
POMP, Wilhelm-Lehmbruck-Museum, Duisburg (D) (Cat.)
2006
an räumen, Galerie Kolster at HdBI, Frankfurt am Main (D)
2002
the drawing roomp./vivvar./bagheria, Kunsthaus Essen (D)
2000
Karin Hochstatter, Galerie Kolster, Frankfurt am Main (D)
1998/99
Salonstücke 7, Städtische Galerie Villa Zanders, Bergisch Gladbach (D) (Cat.)
1998
Lookleftlookright, Hering Raum, Bonn (D) (Cat.)
1996
Karin Hochstatter, Kunstverein Region Heinsberg e. V. (D)
1995
Karin Hochstatter (with Tina Haase), Mannheimer Kunstverein (D) (Cat.)
1994
Karin Hochstatter, ETcetera Galerie im Landesmuseum Mainz (D)
1993
Karin Hochstatter, Brandstetter & Wyss Gallery, Zurich (CH)
1992
Karin Hochstatter, Galerie Ulrich Mueller, Cologne (D)
1991
Karin Hochstatter, Artothek Köln, Cologne (D)
1990
Karin Hochstatter, Derick-Baegert-Gesellschaft, Schloss Ringenberg, Hamminkeln (D)

Selected Group Exhibitions

2020
Optimierung, DGfE-Kongress, Universität zu Köln, Cologne (D) (Cat.)
2019
Animationen, Künstlerverein Malkasten, Düsseldorf (D)
Wechselspiel, Pforzheim Galerie (D) (Cat.)
Point in time, Ekwc, Heusden (NL)
ParanoseProduction, Tina Haase and Karin Hochstatter, film screening, Kunstmuseum Villa Zanders, Bergisch Gladbach (D)
2018
Konvolution, Osthaus Museum Hagen (D)
EWVA, Billboards, Public Space, Cologne (D)
Landschaffen, Project, Montag Stiftung Bonn (D)
den Januarpfad eben, Pade e. V., Alte Kämmerei, Düsseldorf (D)
2017
Strichstärke, Petersburger, Cologne (D)
Heimat?!, Deutscher Künstlerbund e. V., Berlin (D)
Rauschen|Immersion, Edition Basel 2017, Basler Papiermühle (CH)
Wahnsinn, Kunstgruppe Salon Schmitz, Cologne (D)
pull off-breakdown, Gebäudeteil 1, Cologne (D)
2016
Was tun mit der Zeit, Regionale17, Kunstverein Freiburg e. V. (D)
mes amis, mes amies, Sammlung Desgranges, Projektraum Dorrit Nebe, Cologne (D)
Vor der Skulptur, Galerie Ulrich Mueller, Cologne (D)
2015
construct!, Projektraum Deutscher Künstlerbund e. V., Berlin (D)
Avant la Devantgarde, Pade e. V., Düsseldorf (D)
2014
Der haltlose Blick – The Unsteady Gaze, documentation about Karin Hochstatter, Kölner Filmhaus, Cologne (D)
Schlecker, Projektraum Prenzlauer Allee, Berlin (D)
2013
Moiras Planschränke – eingeräumte Zeit, Raketenstation Hombroich, Neuss (D)
Almabrieb, Filmscreening: Haase/Hochstatter, Exhibition Tina Haase, Lädeli, Basel (CH)
Edition: Eins von Hundert, Kunst- & Museumsbibliothek, Museum Ludwig, Cologne (D)
2012
Kunstfilmtag 4, Künstlerverein Malkasten, Düsseldorf (D) (Cat.)
Salonstücke reloaded, Städtische Galerie Villa Zanders, Bergisch Gladbach (D) (Cat.)
Vorgebirgsparkskulptur, Vorgebirgspark, Cologne (D) (Cat.)
2011
Rotterdam VHSfestival, Kunst & Komplex, Rotterdam (NL)
Wenn es ernst wird, Prozesskunst als Konzept. IIB, Raketenstation Hombroich, Neuss (D)
57. Internationale Kurzfilmtage Oberhausen (D)
2010
Kunstfilmtag 3, Künstlerverein Malkasten, Düsseldorf (D) (Cat.)
Esel-lese-filme (with Mechthild Hagemann), vierwände kunst, Düsseldorf (D)
2009
Kunstfilmtag 2, Künstlerverein Malkasten, Düsseldorf (D) (Cat.)
2008
2...3/4_, Raum für Kunst und Musik Köln, Cologne (D)
Fieber tief in den Taschen, Schloss Waldthausen, Mainz (D) (Cat.)
Unter freiem Himmel 1 und 2, Klosterstraße, Botschaft, Düsseldorf (D)
Smaak en Kraak, Keramiekcentrum Tiendschuur Tegelen (NL)

2007
Variation der Wiederholung, Galerie Ulrich Mueller, Cologne (D)
Nachfüllpackung, vierwände kunst, WP8 e. V., Düsseldorf (D)
2006
Body in the Blue, Halle Elektron, Breda (NL)
Body in the Blue, film programme, Künstlerverein Malkasten, Düsseldorf (D)
Förderer fördern, HBK Hochschule für Bildende Künste Braunschweig (D)
2005
20, Kunstverein Region Heinsberg e. V. (D) (Cat.)
2004
Gewalt_Macht_Spaß, Evangelische Staatsakademie, Frankfurt am Main (D)
2003
Arche Noah, Galerie Gabriele Rivet, Cologne (D)
2002
Jeder zeigt ..., Galerie im Brückenturm, Mainz (D)
2001
öffnen-sichern-speichern unter, Tony Wüthrich Galerie, Basel (CH)
Blickwechsel, Galerie Ulrich Mueller, Cologne (D)
Formen der Gewalt, Galerie Gabriele Rivet, Cologne (D)
2000
Die Räder waren unsere Pferde ..., Museum Katharinenhof Kranenburg (D)
Meeting (with Nicola Schrudde), The Tannery Studios, London (UK)
1999
Positionen 33 Painting, Hering Raum, Stahlwerk Willich (D)
Heimat, Galerie Mergemeier, Düsseldorf (D)
1998
Unterschiedliche Dinge, Goethe-Universität Frankfurt am Main, DAZ Deutsches Architektur Zentrum, Berlin (D)
Stadtkunst, Bonn (D) (Cat.)
Tina Haase, Karin Hochstatter, Birgit Werres, Kunstverein Köln rechtsrheinisch e. V. (D) (Cat.)
1997
Labor: Pop, Forum Bildender Künstler Essen (D) (Cat.)
Rohbau, installations in a residential building, Büsdorf (D)
1996
Nähe und Ferne, Stadtmuseum Sofia (BG) (Cat.)
1995
Presentation, Colegio Oficial de Arquitectos de Málaga (E)
Zweiundzwanzig, Bonner Kunstverein (D) (Cat.)
1993
Maltijd, Stichting De Verschijning, Tilburg (NL)
1992
Jahresgaben, Kölnischer Kunstverein, Cologne (D)
1991
X, Orangerie Schloß Brühl (D) (Cat.)
Außerhalb von mittendrin, nGBK neue Gesellschaft für bildende Kunst, e. V., Berlin (D) (Cat.)
Focus Holland, Rheinauen Utrecht (NL) (Cat.)
1990
Peter-Mertes-Stipendiaten, Bonner Kunstverein (D) (Cat.)
1989
Ständegegenstände, Flottmann-Hallen Herne (D) (Cat.)
1988
Lehnskulpturen, Brühler Kunstverein e. V. (D)
1986
Kunstakademie Düsseldorf at Jan van Eyck Academie, Kruisherenklooster, Maastricht (NL)

Curations

2020
Strichstärke², Kunstwerk, Cologne (D)
2019
EWVA-Billboards Edition No2, Deutscher Künstlerbund e. V., Berlin (D)
EWVA-StudioTalks, Cologne (D)
2018/19
Short Visibles II, film programme Moltkerei Werkstatt e. V., Cologne, Kunstmuseum Villa Zanders, Bergisch Gladbach, Pforzheim Galerie, Wacker Kunst, Mühltal (D)
2017
Strichstärke, Petersburger, Cologne (D)
2016
Short visibles I, film programme Markgräflerhof, Basel (CH)
2008
Lückicht, Wandelhalle 1, Städtische Galerie Villa Zanders, Bergisch Gladbach (D)
2006
Spin off, film programme WP8 e. V., Düsseldorf (D)
2005
minidoublemumble, film programme WP8 e. V., Düsseldorf (D)

Initiatives, Projects

2017
starts *Strichstärke*, drawing exhibition series with Katja Butt
EWVA, Equality for Women in Visual Arts is founded with Annebarbe Kau, Stefanie Klingemann, Sabine Elsa Müller and Christine Reifenberger
1984
ParanoseProduction is founded, the film cooperation with Tina Haase

Bibliography

Monographs

Knorre, Alexander von, in *Ständegegenstände*, exhib. cat. Flottmann-Hallen Herne, 1989.

Malsch, Friedemann, *Karin Hochstatter*, in *Peter-Mertes-Stipendiaten* 1989, exhib. cat. Bonner Kunstverein, 1990.

Gerstner, Tobias, *Karin Hochstatter*, in *X*, exhib. cat., Brühler Kunstverein, 1990.

Stammer, Bea, *Karin Hochstatter*, in *Außerhalb von mittendrin*, exhib. cat. nGbK neue Gesellschaft für bildende Kunst e. V., Berlin, 1991.

Eggenberger, Ursula, *Skulpturskizzen und leichte Objekte*, in Tagesanzeiger Zurich, 8.10.1993.

Jolles, Claudia, *Karin Hochstatter und Barbara Mühlefluh*, in Artforum March 1994.

Stather, Martin, *Leichtigkeit des Sichtbaren*, in *Karin Hochstatter*, exhib. cat. Mannheimer Kunstverein, 1995.

Stittgen, Jens, in *Karin Hochstatter*, exhib. cat. Mannheimer Kunstverein, 1995.

Eckstein, Beate, *Wahrnehmungssprünge*, *in Zweiundzwanzig*, exhib. cat. Bonner Kunstverein, 1995.

Kittelmann, Udo, *Karin Hochstatter*, in *Nähe und Ferne*, exhib. cat. Stadtgalerie Sofia, 1996.

Heinrich, Clemens, in *Labor-Pop*, exhib. cat. Forum Bildender Künstler Essen, 1997.

Oelschlägel, Petra, *Karin Hochstatter*, in *Salonstücke 7*, exhib. cat. Städtische Galerie Villa Zanders, Bergisch Gladbach, 1998.

Taschitzki, Thomas von, in *Tina Haase, Karin Hochstatter, Birgit Werres*, exhib. cat. Kunstverein Köln rechtsrheinisch e. V., 1998.

Müller, Sabine Elsa, *Karin Hochstatter, Tilo Riedel, Frances Scholz, Wolfgang Spanier*, in Kunstforum, vol. 153, 2001.

Dorn, Anja, *Frischhaltefolie, artist monograph*, in Kunstforum, vol. 168, 2004.

Koerver, Jens Peter, *Cluster Camp*, in *Vorgebirgsparkskulptur*, exhib. cat. Cologne, 2012.

Oelschlägel, Petra, *Karin Hochstatter*, in *Salonstücke reloaded*, exhib. cat. Städtische Galerie Villa Zanders, Bergisch Gladbach, 2012.

Feyrer, Gundi, *Karin Hochstatter – streut Licht und Luft ins Namenlose aus Gedanken zusammengebaute Momente*, Figure and Essay, 2013, in *27 dicke Bilder und fliegende Sätze* No. 175, Edition Patrick Frey, Zurich, 2015.

Film Portraits and Radio Features

Bergmann, Rudij, *Karin Hochstatter – Künstlerportrait*, TV: Et Zetera-Magazin SDR3, 1994.

Wester, Christel, *Neue Formen der Kunstvermittlung*, radio feature, WDR5 Scala, 4.1.2009.

Kellerwessel, Ulla, *Karin Hochstatter – Der haltlose Blick*, film portrait, colour, sound, 30 min, premiere 2014 Filmhaus, Cologne, DVD.

Authors

Gundi Feyrer (b. 1956), lives and works in Vienna (A), studied sculpture and performance at the HFBK Hochschule für bildende Künste Hamburg (D) and is a writer, filmmaker, performer and drawer. She has published novels, poetry, radio and theatre plays. She has been awarded with several prizes, recently, in 2018, with the H. C.-Artmann-Preis in Vienna (A). Her latest publication about physics and poetry was published in 2017 by Klever Verlag, Vienna (A). The second part *Tempel des Nichts (Das Zaubern)* will be published in 2020 by Ritter Verlag, Klagenfurt (A).

Thomas Wallraff (b. 1969), lives and works in Cologne (D), studied philosophy, literature and art history at the Universität zu Köln, Cologne (D) and the Rheinische Friedrich-Wilhelms-Universität Bonn (D). He is a novelist, poet and essayist about art and literature. In 2014, he published the novelle *Tacet*.

Impressum | Colophon

Konzeption | Concept
Karin Hochstatter,
Alexandra Espenschied,
Doris Hansmann

Texte | Texts
Gundi Feyrer, Thomas Wallraff

Übersetzung | Translation
Gundi Feyrer, Thomas Wallraff

Lektorat | Copy-editing
Doris Hansmann, Lizzie Gilbert

Gestaltung | Graphic design
Alexandra Espenschied

Lithografie | Image editing
dpi-factory, Krefeld

Produktion | Production management
edition cantz

Druck | Printing
Gutenberg Beuys Feindruckerei GmbH,
Langenhagen

Vertrieb und Marketing |
Distribution and marketing
edition cantz
sales@edition-cantz.de

ISBN 978-3-947563-66-1
Printed in Germany

Erschienen bei | Published by
edition cantz
www.edition-cantz.de

edition cantz

Fotonachweis | Photo credits
Klaus Schmitt S. | pp. 12/13, 15, 30/31
Michael Wittassek S. | pp. 9, 16/17
Ulrich Muntenbeck S. | pp. 74/75, 85

Umschlag | Cover
Doppler, 2019, (detail), digital photography, 35 x 80 cm
Inside front: *Skew 1*, 2019, (detail), photography after photocopies after drawings after prints, 42 x 59.4 cm
Inside back: *Skew 2*, 2019, (detail), photography after photocopies after drawings after prints, 42 x 59.4 cm

S. | p. 2: *DS*, 2012, (detail), installation, drinking straws
S. | p. 3: *NNY*, 2018, (detail), wall installation, embroidery mats, wool
S. | p. 6: *PP*, 2008, installation, tape, carpet, reinforcing edge strips, dimension variable
S. | p. 88: *Phi*, 2016, (detail), video projection, 2 min loop, sound, colour, HD 16:9, various foils, nets, curtains
S. | p. 89: *Vorma*, 2018, video still, video loop 1:47 min, sound, colour, HD 16:9
S. | p. 95: *Alaba*, 2015, (detail), construction nets, dimension variable

Dank an | Thanks to
Sebastian Brandl, Agnes Hochstatter, Frances Scholz, Lu Mettelsiefen, Mirek Balonis und | and Jutta Riedel

Mit Unterstützung von | Supported by

STIFTUNG **KUNSTFONDS**

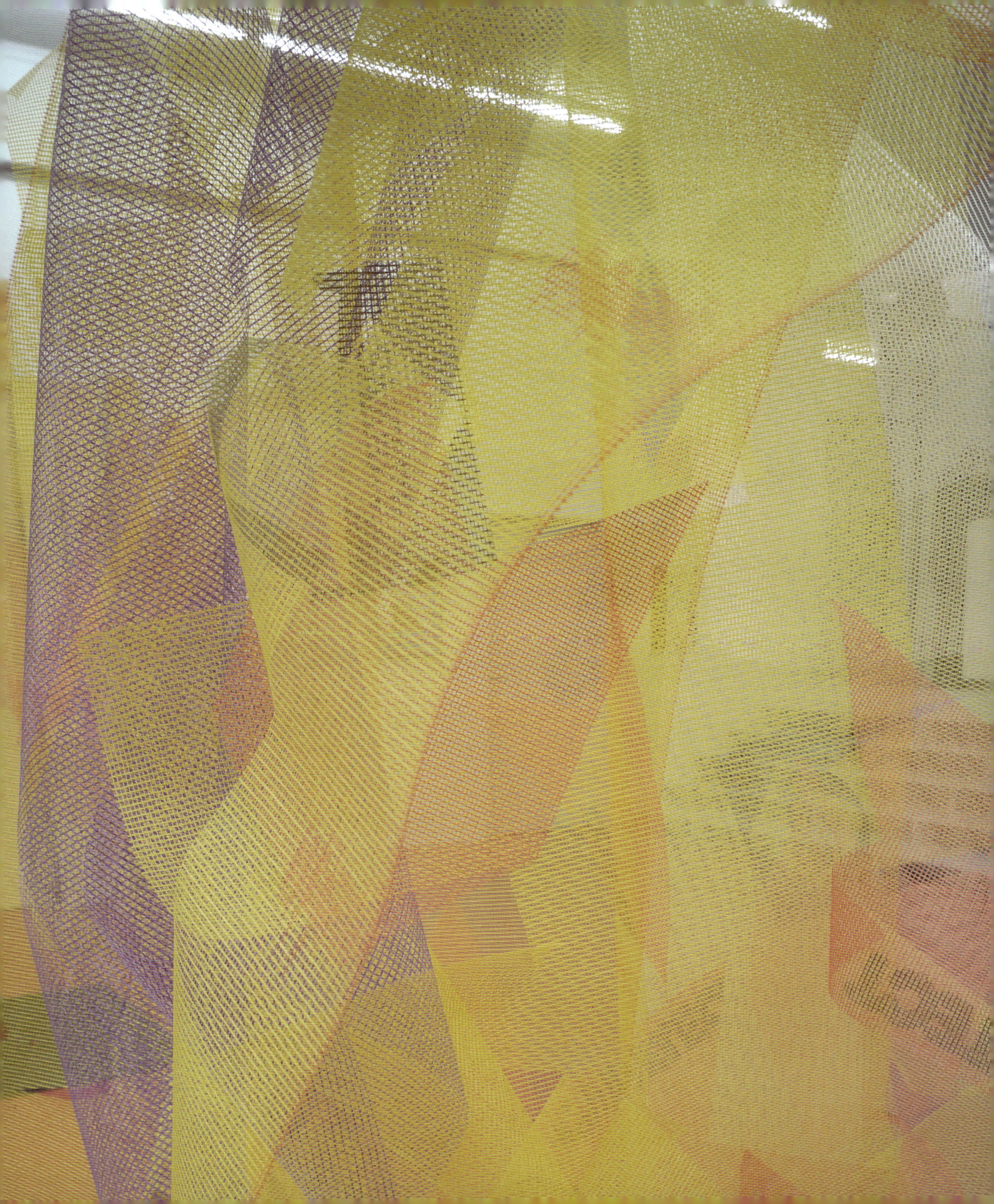